Wet Earth Colliery Scrapbook.

By Dave Lane, Mark Wright & Susan Oliver

GW00673262

2nd Edition August 2014

1

Second Edition   *August 2014*

Published & Distributed by Lulu
www.lulu.com

ISBN   978-1-291-98257-2

Printed in Times New Roman font.

Preface to the Second Edition.

Only two major books have ever been written about Wet Earth Colliery at Clifton, near Manchester. The first one was written by A G Banks and R B Schofield in 1968 – an engineering study of what was at that time visible on the surface at the colliery site in the Irwell Valley. This was the book that introduced many local people to the coal mine at Wet Earth and is still viewed by many as the "classic" book on the subject. The book however contained very little detail about what lay underground at the colliery and much of the underground content was based on theory and speculation.

In 1990, a group of local history and mining enthusiasts started to excavate some of the industrial history sites at Wet Earth, and over a period of many years, our knowledge of the colliery increased considerably.

To record the information gathered by the "Wet Earth Exploration Group, two fairly short publications were written and placed on the internet for free download. These two publications "Wet Earth Scrapbook" by Dave Lane and "Diary of Exploration" by Mark Wright became amazingly popular and were downloaded by many people. Since the initial appearance of these free books, there were many requests for printed versions so the two publications were combined and were published in 2007 as one A4 sized volume as "The Wet Earth Colliery – The Complete Guide".

It's now 2014 and time for a new edition of the book so this volume has been produced – this time in a handier size. It contains all the original material plus a few extra articles and photographs about the Colliery and the surrounding area.

This is our contribution to helping increase knowledge of the local history and heritage of Wet Earth Colliery/

Dave Lane & Mark Wright
August 2014
dave@daveweb.co.uk

Clifton Country Park

How to get there

By car: Clifton Country Park is located just off the A666, Manchester Road between Clifton & Kearsley. The main car park is closed at dusk with 24 hour parking in the overflow car park.

By Bus: Bus numbers: 8 & 22. A bus stop is located approximately .25 miles from the park at Clifton Cricket Ground. For more information contact the GMPTE on 0870 6082608

Car Parking & disabled access: Car Parks are accessed via Clifton House Road. There is a hard surfaced path around the lake providing a circular walk which is fully accessible for disabled users including those in motorised wheelchairs. Three designated parking bays are available for disabled users in the main car park.

Contacts:

Salford Ranger Team,
Clifton Country Park
Clifton House Road
Clifton
Salford
M27 6NG

Telephone: 0161 793 4219

e-mail: clifton.countrypark@salford.gov.uk

Web Site: www.salford.gov.uk/cliftoncountrypark

Opening times: Variable dependent on time of year and staffing levels! See notice board at the visitor centre or the internet for details.

Diary of Exploration

Wet Earth Colliery

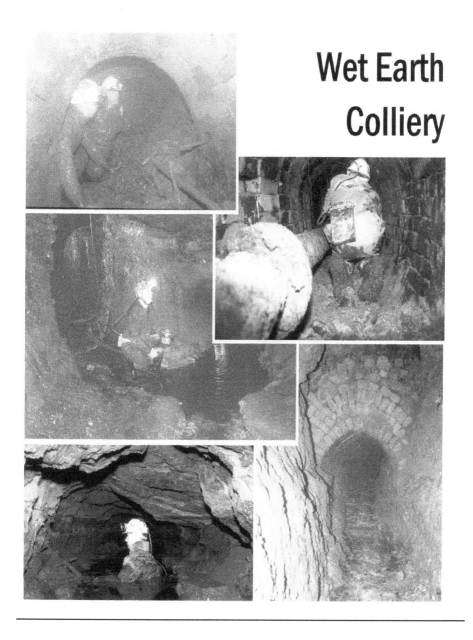

This document has been compiled by Mark Wright and represents the first draft of a publication which will document work carried out by the Wet Earth Colliery Exploration Group.

The group was set up by Alan Davies, Curator of the Lancashire Mining Museum, in order to carry out underground exploration of the colliery drainage scheme.

Over the last five years, changes to local authority and coal authority politics have sadly seen withdrawal of access to the drainage scheme. Due to recent closure of the Lancashire Mining Museum, access to local colliery records or documents relating to WECEG's activities is now virtually impossible.

This 'diary' has been written to ensure that interested parties can gain access to the groups photographs and maps and hopefully carry on the investigation into this fascinating site.

It is not intended as a technical journal, it is merely a desperate attempt to make sure that a record of our work remains available for general use rather than buried in our own filing systems.

The photographs used in this document are just part of a huge collection of slide, negative, digital and video records that have been compiled over a ten year period and were taken mainly by Alan Davies on behalf of the group, and by myself as a group member.

If you want more information or need to make a comment, don't hesitate to get in touch.

Contact me as the author by email on BCONFINED@aol.com or look at Dave Lanes Wet Earth Colliery web site on the internet.

Mark Wright   January 2003

Introduction

The national and historical importance of Wet Earth Colliery is due primarily to the work of James Brindley who achieved fame in the 18th Century as a canal engineer.

His solution to the water problems at the colliery remains unique in the annals of coal mining history and provides us with an insight into the genius with which he was to approach other, better documented projects.

Poorly described by contemporary historians, the rise and fall of Wet Earth Colliery is briefly described in the following notes:-

The Irwell Valley Fault follows the course of the River Irwell in a North East to South West direction and is a 3000ft downthrow of strata with rocks known as the Permian Measures overlying the coal measures north of the fault.

On the Southern (Clifton) bank of the river we find coal outcropping close to the surface; whereas on the Northern (Ringley) bank the same seams are almost 3000ft below.

It is likely that at an early date the outcropping seams would have been discovered and mined on a small scale, probably by bell pits or drift mines, but these would have been quickly worked out and of little commercial use.

It was not until 1740 when John Heathcote, a gentleman landowner, sank the first 'deep' mine on site, that major efforts were made to win coal.

Heathcote employed Matthew Fletcher, a mining engineer whose father and brother were both involved in mining, and looked forward to the prosperity which the coal would bring. This prosperity was unfortunately thwarted by water which flooded the mine soon after completion.

Even with the aid of his father and brother, Fletcher was unable to effect the necessary drainage and so, in 1750 the up and coming James Brindley was called upon for advice.

Tales regarding the meeting between Heathcote, Brindley and Fletcher appear to have been romanticised over the years but nonetheless, in 1752 Brindley was credited with the construction of a weir at Ringley.

From it he drove a passage some 800yd to a point opposite the colliery albeit on the wrong side of the river.

Working to an imaginative plan, Brindley led the water into an inverted siphon ('U' bend) discharging onto the southern bank of the Irwell.

The flowing water was then channelled along a stream bed to the colliery where it continued to a large chamber adjacent to the pit shaft itself.

Here it drove a wooden water wheel which in turn operated pumps that eventually drained the workings. Both drive water and pumped water were taken away from the wheel chamber via a tailrace which discharged back to the river.

Granted a new lease of life the colliery prospered and in 1790 Matthew Fletcher, now landowner, began to extend Brindley's feeder stream to link with the Manchester, Bolton and Bury Canal in readiness for the latter opening to traffic in 1801.

Access to a wider market generated expansion at Wet Earth and in 1804 the purchase of a steam engine was coupled with the sinking of a second shaft to signify a new era.

By 1860, control of the mining interests had passed from the Fletcher family to Joseph and Josiah Evans who had extensive holdings in the Haydock area.

Along with their nephews, the Pilkington Brothers, they formed the Clifton & Kersley Coal Company and sank a third shaft. Initially it was used as a furnace ventilation shaft but in 1898 this dangerous practise was superseded when a ventilation fan was purchased and installed at the pit-head.

Between 1880 and 1900 there was a strong investment in surface plant.

Coal screening equipment and a railway yard were constructed to deal with increased production from deeper seams and in 1901 compressed air rope haulage was installed to replace the use of ponies below ground.

Between 1900 and 1917 many seams became exhausted and after the 1921 coal-strike, only the plodder re-opened.

In 1928 economics finally signified the closure of Wet Earth Colliery and in 1929 the Clifton and Kersley Coal Company ceased to exist, having amalgamated with other local collieries to form the Manchester Collieries Limited.

Lying derelict, the colliery was amazingly saved from industrial re-development and in 1958 two engineers, A.G. Banks and R.B. Schofield, were drawn to the site thus acting as a catalyst for the interest which has consumed me for the last fifteen years, and latterly for the project detailed within this report.

Mark D. Wright
May 1993

Chapter One - Setting the Scene

Clifton is approximately half way between Manchester and Bolton and some five miles from its more famous counterpart of Worsley.

Having recently been described by the tourism chiefs from Salford City Council as an 'idyllic river valley' it appears a complete contrast to the scene 60 years ago.

In 1928, two years after the General Strike and during the subsequent depression, Clifton, primarily a coal mining area was badly hit.

Mines were in private ownership and profits had to be forthcoming both for owners and shareholders.

On 2nd February 1928 at a meeting of the directors, it was decided that Wet Earth Colliery was no longer profitable and it was resolved that:-

In consequence of the present unsatisfactory market conditions and despite the low wages cost per ton, that Wet Earth Colliery be closed forthwith and until further notice..........[1]

Thus ended the life of what was possibly the longest working pit in the area.

---

[1] Salford Mining Museum, Clifton & Kersley Coal Co Minute Book, Ref 131-133 2/2/1928

Closure did not immediately entail the removal of the pit buildings as it does today, rather the opposite.

Buildings and especially the shafts were left intact in the hope that economics would justify the mines being re-opened.

The latter day use of early shafts at the nearby Agecroft Colliery is a prime example of such an occurrence.

It has been said that buildings were still standing at Wet Earth Colliery even as late as 1945 but we have to admit that there are no records to support this comment.

Written evidence is particularly scarce due to the fact that about 20 years after closure of the colliery a large number of original records were destroyed by the estates management office.

Nobody could really say what was lost but without doubt, little survives today!

Factories, power stations and housing have appeared within the vicinity of Wet Earth Colliery although, with the exception of the M62 motorway which cuts across the eastern side of the site, both industrial and domestic redevelopment have left the colliery virtually unscathed.

Huge amounts of ballast were required by the motorway contractors and a suitable source was discovered at Clifton in 1967.

Although the gravel extraction fortuitously avoided the main colliery area the scale of operation can be seen even today in the form of a lake which is by far one of the most dominant features of the area.

Previous to this, the National Coal Board attempted to landscape the derelict site by planting a profusion of trees and, although an admirable gesture in 1964, the near 30 year old trees are now creating conflict between arboriculturist and industrial archaeologist! By 1966, management of local river valleys had passed into control of the Croal Irwell Valley Conference[2].

Involving Lancashire County Council and the former boroughs of Salford and Bolton, the conference identified three major objectives;

- to improve the valley environment
- to improve public access
- to improve the scope for recreational use

Between 1966 and 1973 much progress was made in stimulating the public's awareness towards the valley. They were told to look after and enjoy the countryside on their doorstep and by 1979 few could deny that they had heard of the Croal Irwell Valley.

A report on the Greater Manchester County, Croal Irwell Local Plan stated in 1979 that 'Clifton House Farm offers potential for a variety

[2] GMC Croal Irwell Valley report of surveys and issues, June 1979, page 3

of recreational uses; these should be primarily quiet and informal, incorporating local history'[3]

Although the quiet and informal use of the Clifton House Farm site was immediately implemented via a countryside warden service, it was not until 1988 that official interest was properly channelled to include local history.

Between 1979 and 1987 Clifton House Farm was firmly established on the North West leisure scene.

Tree planting and grading around the lake provided suitable habitat for a variety of birds whilst stocking the waters with fish was welcomed by local angling groups; walkers found the well defined nature trails and paths were easy to follow.

Every group was catered for except the local historian.

Poor woodland management now meant that trees were growing less than 3ft away from each other. Decaying timbers lay beneath the branches of saplings whilst blackberry bushes quickly filled any remaining spaces.

Neglect had created a veritable jungle making any form of survey impossible and amongst all this 'nature', only the knowledgeable individual would be able to trace the vague remains of Wet Earth Colliery.

---

[3] GMC Croal Irwell Valley report of surveys and issues, June 1979, page 65

BY the mid-1980's a movement had arisen to make people aware of their urban heritage and one local result of this was the Greater Manchester Archaeological Unit being commissioned to excavate a cottage below Dixon Fold.

The location of the cottage was known although pit waste and undergrowth covered the whole area making it impossible to find the remains without careful searching.

A successful operation revealed the foundations and today the walls have been restored to a height of about 4ft. Under similar conditions, the colliery locomotive shed was tidied up and here luck prevailed with timber sleepers being revealed beneath the pit waste.

By June 1990 the cycle of destruction that started in 1928 had turned a full circle.

The green movement had prospered causing leisure and open spaces to become politically important and in the face of possible local re-organisation the idea of a country park scheme was adopted.

The old terminology of 'Clifton House Farm Site' was abandoned in favour of the current title 'Clifton Country Park' and amidst this political scenario, Alan Davies, Museum Officer at Salford Mining Museum was consulted regarding interpretation of the site.

Being in a far better position to advise on historical and archaeological background than the planners at council level he was immediately able to assess the situation and offer long term guidance.

Within a matter of months he brought together a group of enthusiasts and formed the 'Wet Earth Colliery Exploration Group' (WECEG) who were briefed to delve deeper into the fascinating if somewhat frustrating remnants of Wet Earth Colliery.

Photograph showing the original party proceeding upstream towards Giants Seat

Chapter Two – Previous Research

Although many have attempted to recount the history of the mine it has long been established that few contemporary records exist which give reference to Wet Earth Colliery.

As long ago as 1795, Aiken[4], gave quite a detailed account in his work. Smiles[5] gave further discourse to the subject in 1861 whilst Corbett[6] followed in 1907.

More recently comment has been made by Boucher[7]; Sheard & Hurst[8] and Bode[9] but undoubtedly the most thorough study to have been published is that by Banks & Schofield[10] in 1968.

To date the Banks & Schofield study has remained the definitive work bringing together research of local historians and the engineering knowledge of the joint authors.

Extensive field work provided Banks & Schofield with a set of surveys that accurately portrayed visible remains as they *were between 1958 and* 1968.

In addition to such published work it was known that the site had attracted individuals who carried out their own research, most of which had fortunately been deposited with local institutions and has been traced for use in the current project[11].

In conjunction with numerous field trips an examination of this available data confirmed that major surface features at Wet Earth Colliery would have to remain out of reach for the time being.

---

[4] Aiken J, A description of the country from 30 to 40 miles around Manchester, 1795

[5] Smiles S, Lives of the engineers with an account of their principle works, 1861, pages 322-324

[6] Corbett J, The River Irwell, 1907, pages 74-75

[7] Boucher C, James Brindley Engineer 1716-1772, 1968

[8] Sheard RL & KG Hurst, History of water problems in the South Lancs Coalfield, Mining Engineer, August/September 1973

[9] Bode H, James Brindley an Illustrated Life, pages 11-14

[10] Banks AG & RB Schofield, Brindley at Wet Earth Colliery, 1968

[11] Beswick D and MD Wright, 1970's to mid 1980's

Similarly it was concluded that the underground aspect of Brindleys drainage scheme had previously been ignored even with 19 adits (allocated an alphabetical code for ease of reference) being accessible on the river bank between Giants Seat and the M62 motorway bridge.

The close proximity of the mine to these adits, coupled with standard practise of draining workings via soughs, suggested that one or more of the adits would possibly be linked to the colliery itself.

On 16 June 1990 the first meeting of WECEG took place with a 13 strong team assembling on site.

Archaeologist, geologist, historian and conservationist were present as a cross section representing the diversity of interests that were concerned for the future success of Clifton Country Park.

The party set off with a clear objective in mind.

To explore a tunnel said by Banks & Schofield to drain the colliery dry dock, and although nothing formal had been arranged it was hoped to determine whether or not the tunnel was of greater importance.

Doubt had been cast on Banks & Schofields findings when preliminary exploration in the 1980's revealed that the tunnel continued far beyond its supposed end[12].

---

[12] Beswick D and MD Wright

Chapter Three – The First Survey of Tunnel E (main tunnel)

Entry to the system was gained through a broken grille which ironically had been placed originally to prevent unauthorised access.

The warm air above ground was immediately replaced by the cool, surprisingly fresh air within the tunnel.

Natural ventilation appeared to be functioning correctly somewhat dispelling the fear that noxious gases would be present.

Within feet of the entrance a square shaft had been set into the roof and although a solid capping prevented confirmation it is almost certain that this was a drain for one section of Fletchers Canal.

First impressions were of a tunnel far too large, even allowing for the cheapness of eighteenth century labour, to have been used merely for drainage purposes.

True floor level was obscured by a covering of silt but even so it was estimated that the tunnel would have been some 6ft high by 4ft wide.

Pick marks were visible in the soft sandstone and their angle of cut indicated that the tunnel had been driven from the river bank rather than from the colliery.

The following pages detail some of the features noted along the main tunnel route.

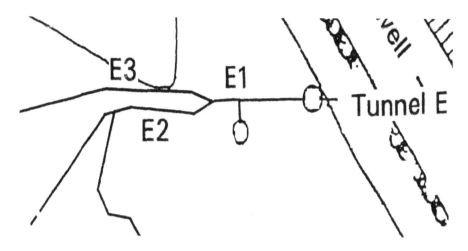

Two passages, E1 and E2 ran to the left of the main tunnel. Both were of square section and cut fairly high above the silt floor level.

E1 soon ended at a circular shaft which had been capped less than 18 inches above the tunnel roof level. The floor beneath the shaft comprised a soft silt  material which may have been infill indicating that either the shaft continued to a lower level, or there had been constant erosion due to a large frequent water flow.

Due to estimated distance, positioning and comparison with the ordnance survey maps it appeared that tunnel E1 had been the tunnel serving the drydock and boatyard.

E2 proved to be much longer running uphill before bifurcating.

The larger passage turned at 90 degrees and ran for some distance before coming

to an abrupt end. A smaller passage ran ahead quickly becoming silted to within inches of roof level.

Back in the main tunnel, brickwork was visible in the right hand wall indicating that a shaft or passage had been sealed, E3.

Intriguingly the handmade bricks had been laid to form a slight curve, possibly taking pressure from whatever lay beyond.

Tunnel E (main tunnel) changed shape from a 'pointed' roof to a 'flat' roof as it drew close to the Irwell Valley Fault zone. Both views are looking inbye.

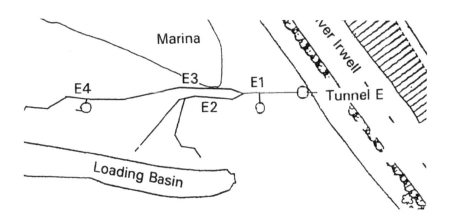

A large square chamber, E4, had been cut to the left of the main tunnel. The chamber was separated from yet another tunnel by a partly collapsed brick wall but deep silt below 2ft of ochre stained water prevented investigation.

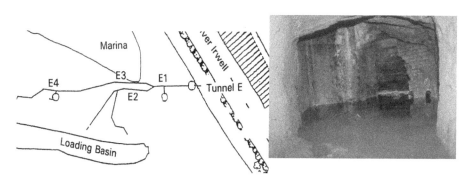

A square section shaft had been cut through the sandstone, the upper section being brick lined. A corrugated capping was visible.

Approximately 20ft beyond E4 a heavy clay deposit could be seen on the right hand side of the passage.

The angle of the tunnel walls at this point indicated that there was possibly a mouthing behind the clay stopping.

The main tunnel itself took on a different form becoming brick lined with frequent changes in direction, possibly indicating that we were now inside the Irwell Valley Fault zone.

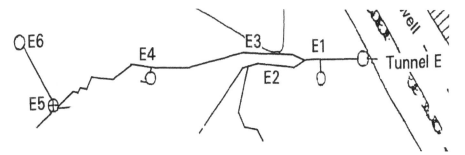

As the brick lined section gave way to shale it was apparent that we were within the Irwell Valley Fault Zone.

Approximately 15m into the shale section the tunnel was obstructed by a mass of steelwork and rubble

From the roof of the tunnel a small diameter shaft, E5, led to the surface.

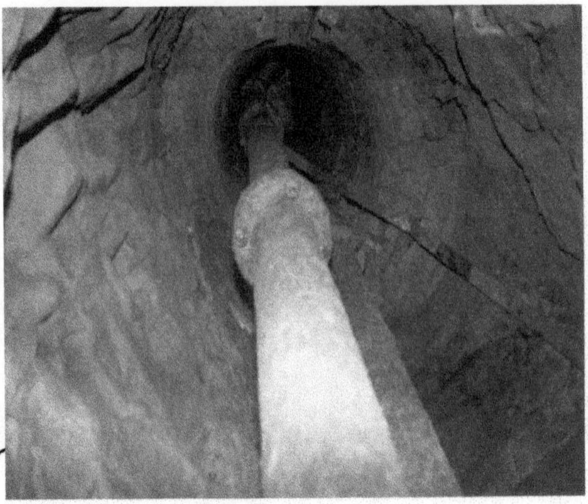

Of great interest were two pipes which stood vertical in the shaft.

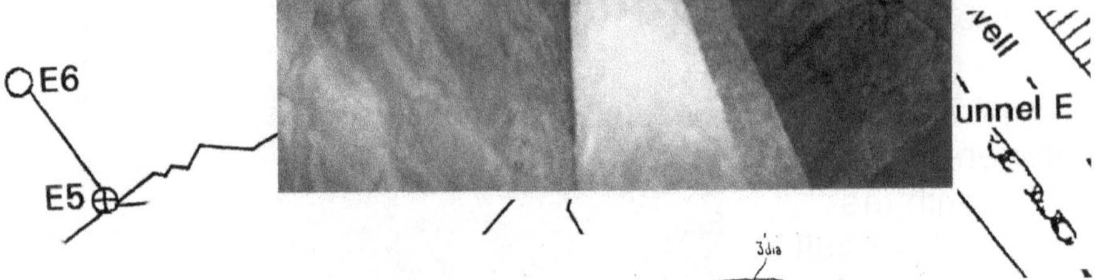

E6

E5

Sketch detailing layout of the pump shaft E5 (taken from a survey by Weston and Smith in 1971)

Tunnels could be seen to left and right of the main tunnel.

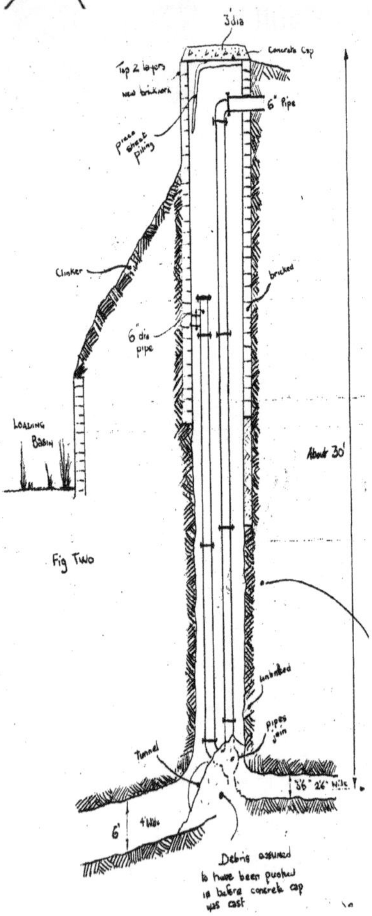

The right hand tunnel, E6, appeared to run uphill with a rock floor mostly covered in a sticky ochre clay.

View from E5 into E6 with an 'explorer' travelling back down towards E5.

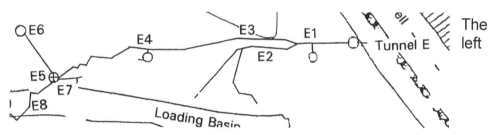

hand tunnel, E7, ran slightly downwards having a sloped roof supported on its right by a random packed stone wall.

View looking from E5 towards E7.

Within 20ft of dropping into the left hand tunnel, E7, the section opened into a large tunnel which became brick lined in the distance.

At the same point a small brick lined passage entered from the right but once again deep ochre stained water prevented further exploration.

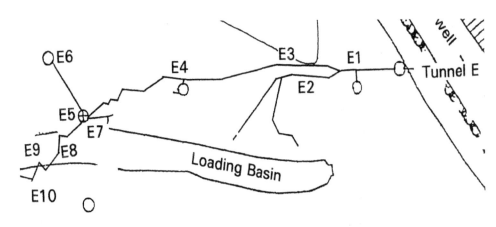

Moving inbye from the pump shaft E5, the strata continued as shale.

Confirming the weakness of the surrounding rock, rails had been inserted across the tunnel as roof supports, E8.

Having travelled below the loading basin a further three rails supported the roof in front of what could only be described as a brick doorway, E9.

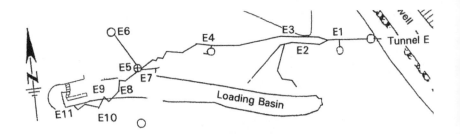

Still working
through the shale,
the tunnel
appeared to
continue ahead
although a large
deposit of silt and
fireclay prevented
exploration, E10.

The main tunnel
seemed to end at a
collapsed brick wall
which, on investigation,
proved to be a high
circular shaft
constructed from
dressed stone blocks,
E11.

An arched passage
formed the top part of
the shaft whilst a random stone wall sealed the whole area.

This location had been surveyed and drawn by Banks & Schofield &
was immediately identified as the side weir from the colliery loading
basin.

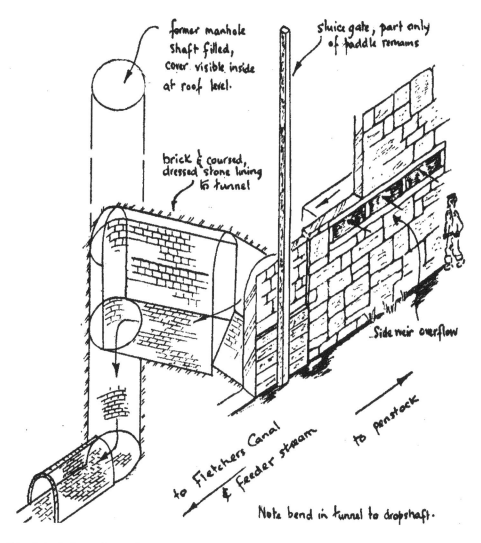

In the sketch:
- former manhole shaft filled, cover visible inside at roof level.
- sluice gate, part only of paddle remains
- brick & coursed, dressed stone lining to tunnel
- Side weir overflow
- to Fletchers Canal & feeder stream
- to penstock
- Note bend in tunnel to dropshaft.

Sketch taken from Brindley at Wet Earth Colliery (Banks & Schofield) detailing the 'overflow weir & drop shaft in loading basin' as seen in 1965

Undoubtedly a valuable exercise, the first survey proved that tunnel E was of considerable importance and hinted that much would probably be revealed by a more detailed examination of the adjacent tunnels.

Chapter Four – The Next Stage

Work was soon underway to reveal more about the system and a breakthrough came with the discovery of a survey completed by two Salford University students who had explored tunnel E and its adjacent areas in 1971[13].

Their report echoed our initial findings and, along with a detailed map, indicated that nothing below ground appeared to have changed between 1971 and 1990.

From the outset it was obvious that the pump shaft, E4, begged attention and after a search on the north side of the basin, Wes Halton, the country park warden was able to locate its buried capping.

Below ground the shaft and its environs had been largely cleared of infill thus revealing more of the pipework whilst at the same time allowing many gallons of water to drain into the lower lying left hand tunnel, E7.

Bearing in mind the amount of water flowing along this new route (a slight flow was also observed coming from the

---

[13] SMM, A survey & investigation of the spillway tunnel carried out in the early months of 1971, Smith JC and DP Weston

small brick lined passage) it was surprising that there was no appreciable rise in the water level along its length.

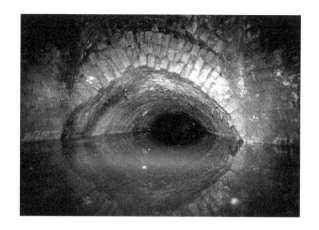

Small tunnel to the right of E7 given the name 'ochre canal'.

The fact that flooding didn't occur was an interesting point which indicated that there could be an outlet in the distance or even that the system was so extensive it could easily absorb the additional fluid.

It was an intrepid pair who eventually entered the water in an attempt to solve the mystery.

The unspoken hope was to exit on the river bank but with ochry silt quickly reaching waist height, success seemed a long way off.

On leaving the junction with E7, several notable features were observed[14].

---

[14] Alan Davies & Mark Wright, 1990

What had appeared to be a large pipe running across the tunnel was in fact a timber support preventing the lined walls from collapsing inwards.

Although initially difficult movement became easier inside the brick lined section where a solid floor could be felt beneath the silt.

The tunnel lining did not remain constant for the whole of its length and underwent three changes in dimension before it entered a strata of good sandstone.

At its start the lining was seven bricks deep giving a narrow almost 'conduit' feel to the tunnel.

The first section gave way to a larger area which was essentially lined although the lining had mostly fallen away from the surrounding strata revealing a depth of only one brick.

Once again, the tunnel became lower, this time due to a lining five bricks thick.

The tunnel changed height several times and as the brick lining ended, the section passed back into sandstone.

An examination of the immediate area revealed what looked to be a passage going ahead at water level whilst an opening, partly bricked could be seen to the left.

The photos do not really show how bad conditions were inside the tunnel. The semi fluidic silt was waist deep, numbingly cold and 'oozed' into every exposed

part of the body. In a most un-nerving way the silt even found its way into 'hidden' parts of the body!

At this stage we had little idea that the ochre was really quite poisonous!

After several minutes contemplation it was realised with a shock that we were standing in the passage beyond the square chamber, E4, a point which we had previously thought inaccessible due to depth of the ochery silt.

Probing confirmed that a mixture of twigs and silt blocked the entrance to a tunnel which continued at a lower level than the main body of E4 and on the basis of this it seemed reasonable to judge that, with the exception of natural seepage, this lower

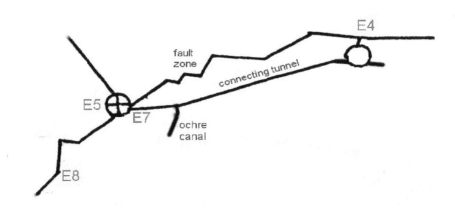

tunnel was the route by which water was draining.

When plotted it became obvious that we had followed a route parallel to, but several feet lower than the main section of tunnel E.

Less obvious however was the reason for such a duplication.

An idea began forming that this could be part of the tailrace passing between the wheel chamber at Wet Earth and the river bank and, although something of a gamble (Banks & Schofield had previously mapped the tailrace to the south east of the loading basin) certain fact appeared to back up this theory.

A bearing taken along the small brick lined tunnel (ochre canal) showed that it headed in the general direction of the main colliery area, the only likely reason for this would be mine drainage.

The foundations for a brick wall were found across the passage E7 indicating that this tunnel had at one time been sealed thus severing the connection with E5 and preventing water from passing back into the main tunnel.

Diagram showing the whole of tunnel E (main tunnel).

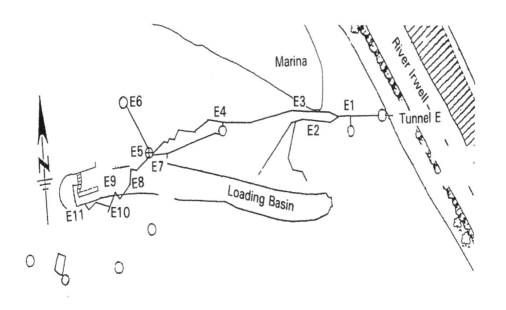

Chapter Five - The Gas House Tunnel

Travelling between the pump shaft, E5, and the junction at E10, it was becoming more and more obvious that there was sometimes a difference in the quality of air, quite often coupled with a lowering of temperature.

A closer inspection of the blockage at this point revealed that the silt was actually a deposit in front of a brick wall which had been constructed across the width of the passage.

Whilst looking for a weak spot cold air could be felt coming from behind the wall and after a little demolition it was possible to get one hand into the gap between masonry and stone.

The flow of air increased noticeably suggesting that an open passage could lie beyond.

Having decided to breach the wall we removed a quantity of silt and began to attack the masonry[15]. Two hours later we had barely made any impact and were on the verge of giving up.

Matters were worsened by deep mud all around the junction, a glutinous substance which had enough power to remove Wellingtons whenever movement was contemplated.

---

[15] Richard Fairhurst, Alan Davies, Mark Wright, 1990

Summoning a final burst of strength we persuaded bricks and mortar to part company only to find another layer beyond.

Anger took over and saw us through the second and then third layer until finally, the chisel broke through to open air.

Exercising our usual caution we moved forwards simultaneously testing for mine gases and oxygen deficiency. Neither were encountered and although the silt deposit reduced headroom to less than 18 inches we made rapid progress for some 65ft.

Here we found that a mixture of rubble, sanitary fittings and pit waste had spread out from the base of a shaft thus blocking our route.

An attempt at clearing the blockage actually caused more material to fall and in view of the limited space available we decided it was safer to abandon the project and retreat to the junction at E10.

By cross referencing our own data with the ordnance survey we were able to plot the position of the latest blockage as being below the former gas house.

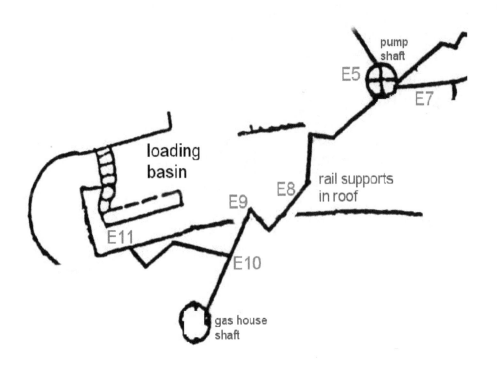

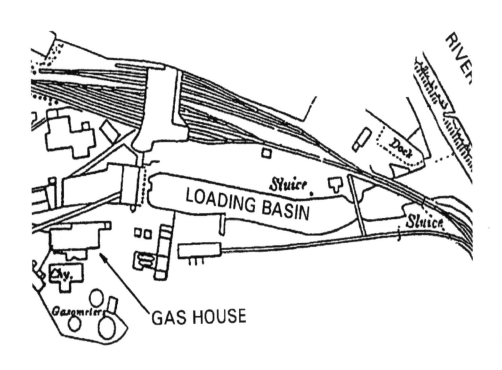

Chapter Six – The Assumed Tailrace (tunnel F)

Following on the theory that we had previously travelled a section of the tailrace it seemed logical that the next course of action would be to locate the tunnel at its opening on the river bank.

This was by far the easiest task to date as Banks & Schofield had already mapped and photographed the entrance[16]. Redesignated as tunnel F, the mouthing was quickly located about 30yds downstream of tunnel E.

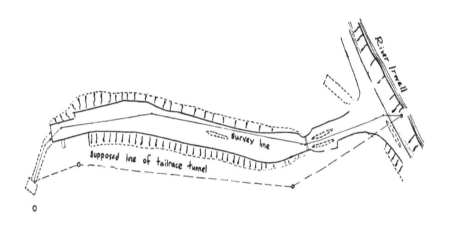

To remain consistent it was decided, with due respect, that until our own survey had been completed[17] we should not accept that the entrance was indeed that of the original tailrace.

Exactly as described by Banks & Schofield the tunnel was almost circular in section and certainly the lowest (height) of the tunnels explored to date.

Conditions underfoot were not too pleasant and forwards motion was only possible via a crab like crawl on hands and knees.

---

[16] Banks, AG and RB Schofield, note 9, 93, 103-105
[17] Mike Shardlow and Richard Fairhurst, 14 July 1990

Coupled with several inches of water and mud this movement resulted in a very dirty explorer!

Almost familiar by now a canal drainage shaft, F1, was passed without difficulty.

Rising slightly the tunnel floor gave way to sandstone and after changing direction we were amazed to find a sudden climb of almost 6ft.

Skirting a blocked off passage, F2, the tunnel at this point became brick lined and, fully expecting it to end in deep silt it was actually quite disturbing to find that some 155ft from the entrance, tunnel F came to an abrupt end in what could be described as an 8ft high brick chamber, F3.

The front of the chamber contained a wooden paddle sluice.

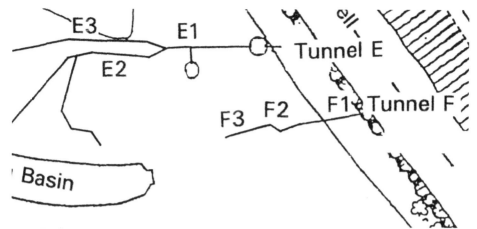

Surface measurements indicated that F3 was located very close to the dry dock entrance where ordnance survey maps readily confirmed the presence of an overflow[18].

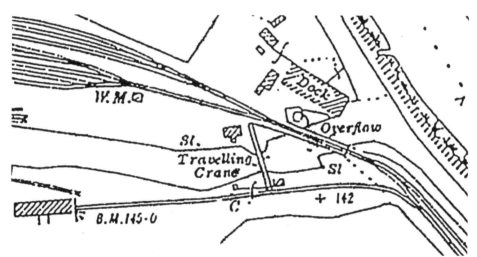

At its end there could be no doubt that tunnel F was travelling well above the height expected of a link with the lower level of the wheel chamber therefore it would be reasonable to suggest that perhaps we were not in the tailrace after all.

---

[18] O.S. 1:2500 County Series Lancashire sheet XCV12, editions of 1907 and 1927 shows feature

Attention quickly turned to tunnel G, the only other tunnel in the immediate vicinity and of no obvious interest.

The tunnel was blocked pretty well to roof height and appeared to be in the correct position for a canal drain.

Forced to examine the tunnel more closely we realised that there was a free passage beyond the silt deposit and it looked a 'fairly simple' task to dig a way through!

Photograph showing the entrance to tunnel G several weeks after entry had been made under the gate.

Chapter Seven – Hard Work & No Answers (tunnel G)

Spirits were somewhat dampened after failing to connect with tunnels E and F so it was a subdued group who began to clear a trench along one side of tunnel G.

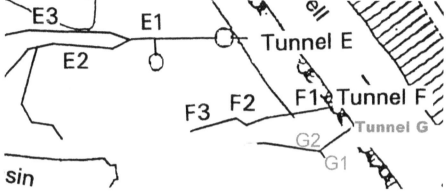

Water could be seen glinting in the distance but the barrier of silt prevented even the smallest person from travelling more than 15ft towards it and, although soft, it was difficult to excavate due to the mass of roots holding it together.

After many hours of work a crosscut saw proved to be the best tool enabling silt to be cut into sections and then carried out of the tunnel by hand.

Gradually becoming deeper and longer the trench passed beyond daylight and it was eventually possible to make out the features of a water filled junction.

A passage crossing tunnel G and apparently running parallel to the river (G1 to the left and G2 to the right).

Spurred on by this new discovery work continued and several weeks later the water was tapped with thousands of gallons being released[19].

Many tons of silt were washed out thus allowing a clear view of the junction G1/G2.

Over the next few weeks the flow of water began to undercut our trench making access difficult (if not dangerous) and eventually it became necessary to remove all of the silt from the first section of tunnel G.
On reaching a solid floor we were faced with a tunnel some 8ft high and 4ft wide. The roof dropped steeply giving a height of only 6ft at the junction.

As in most of the other tunnels along the river bank, grooves had been cut near the entrance to accommodate stop boards. Tunnel G however differed from the norm in two ways.

First of all, three pairs of grooves were visible with the innermost pair being fully preserved.

[19] Alan Davies & Mike Shardlow, August 1990

This revealed the method by which the boards had been inserted & with the discovery of some nails on an adjacent ledge, confirmed that at various times the boards would have been securely fixed, possibly to prevent being dislodged by river water.

Secondly it was noticed that tunnel G was devoid of a connection to Fletchers Canal thereby indicating that the tunnel was probably too important to have been used solely as a canal drain.

The initial force of escaping water slowed to a trickle and it became obvious that we had only tapped liquid that lay on top  of a more solid deposit of silt which had acted as a form of plug.

Resorting to schoolboy methods a process of damming and flushing was adopted in an attempt to progress along G2.

Results were slow in coming but eventually access was possible wearing chest waders. Conditions underfoot were treacherous with the clinging silt making every step a real effort.

It was whilst reaching for support in this section that an unusual feature was noticed.

At regular intervals parallel notches had been cut into both walls of the tunnel providing an almost perfect handhold.

Over a period of weeks we managed to work our way to a brick lined section, G3, but roof and floor practically met at this point forcing us to obtain protective equipment before the survey could continue.

After donning dry suits[20] it was possible to drop into the lined tunnel and take a compass bearing from G3.

This indicated that if the tunnel held its route it would possibly connect with the lower tunnel adjacent to E4.

No more than 20ft in length the lined area gave way to sandstone and within 100ft a side passage, G4, opened to the right at a higher level than the main tunnel.

---

[20] Supplied by John Ledsham, Diving Dept, Manchester Ship Canal Company

Access could be gained to a circular shaft which was almost completely obscured by an infill of timber & loose materials. Adjacent to E4, the main tunnel was once again brick lined, G5, and this reduced the height between water and roof to less than 1 ft.

G4 - Photo taken AFTER removal of the silt

A series of studs could be seen around the brick lining indicating that something, possibly a brattice, had been secured across the tunnel.

The reduced headroom finally prevented us from going ahead and it seemed that little could be done until either the water receded or the silt could be removed.

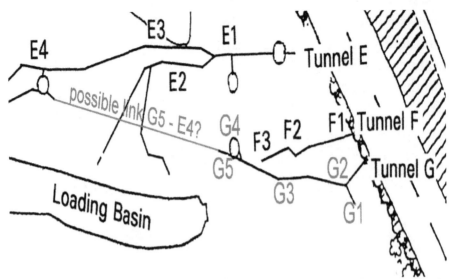

Dealing with the silt appeared to be the lesser of two evils but even so it was estimated that over 400ft of tunnel required attention, a mammoth task that would severely strain the limited manpower available.

Ironically the unfortunate closure of Agecroft Colliery brought a solution in the form of a powerful pump which the colliery management donated for use at Wet Earth[21].

Following Brindleys example of using water against water it was decided to increase the flow along tunnel G to such an extent that the outgoing liquid would carry with it much of the softer silt and, working on the assumption that tunnel G continued to E4, a delivery hose was placed below the water level at the supposed junction.

Our efforts had not been in vain because some 20 minutes after the pump had been activated a large flow of ochre stained water was observed at the entrance to tunnel G.

---

[21] After closure in 1991 the colliery management donated various items for use both at Wet Earth Colliery and Astley Green Colliery museum. Choosing from a list too large to detail fully, the most important items taken to Wet Earth were a Lister pump, suction & delivery hoses and a variety of strainers & nozzles. Without this gracious donation it is most likely that work would have quickly ground to a halt and for that reason we must hold ourselves indebted to the former staff and management at Agecroft Colliery

The boost to morale was short lived with a major problem appearing on the scene.

Where the water had been drained from G2 a deep sticky mud appeared as residue making it difficult to travel beyond G3, in fact the journey became so exhausting that reaching G4 could take up to 15 minutes.

Undoubtedly of our own making the latest difficulty took us back to square one and yet again we were faced with the option of struggling on or removing the silt.

Time after time we found that even a strong flow of water would fail to make a lasting impact on conditions within the tunnel, it would certainly cut a channel but once the flow ceased the silt would merely hang in place.

Becoming totally frustrated at the lack of progress we put in a determined effort and waded against the flow to drag a deep channel using spades and rakes.

Gaining 60ft in less than three hours it was not long before we were level with G4 and within a week it was possible to pass below the lining at G5.

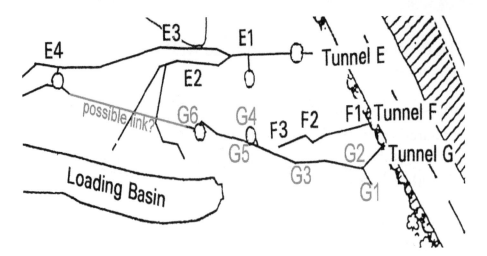

Once inside the lined area it was obvious that the tunnel ahead was of a similar height to the rest of G2 although a solid plug of material had formed a barrier almost 15ft long causing water to build up for quite a distance.

Pushing on for an exhausting 80ft a second shaft was discovered, G6[22].

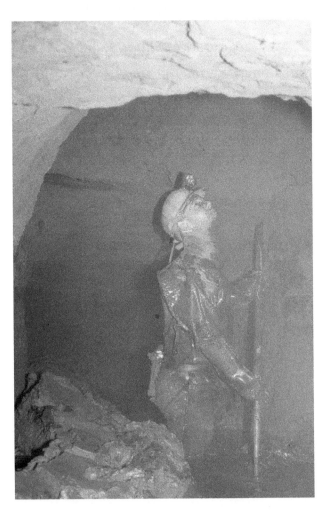

---

[22] Alan Davies 14 August 1991

Views of G6 taken <u>AFTER</u> the silt had been removed

Chapter 8 – Making the Connection

The plug of silt near G5 proved to be some 4ft deep and when breached allowed a tremendous amount of water to be released[23]. Increasing dramatically the flow brought with it more and more silt and amazingly the water changed from dirty black to bright orange.

As every second passed the channel grew wider and deeper. The passage literally opened up in front of us and before the flow subsided we saw the silt level drop by almost 24 inches.

Realising that a major development had taken place somewhere ahead we left tunnel G and moved to the outlet pipe at E4 where the rest of the group were in a highly excited state.

---

[23] Matthew Smith & Mark Wright, 17 August 1991

The square chamber, E4, had drained almost completely and a raging torrent from the direction of E7 was rapidly disappearing into an opening that had appeared where we had previously suspected the existence of a lower tunnel.

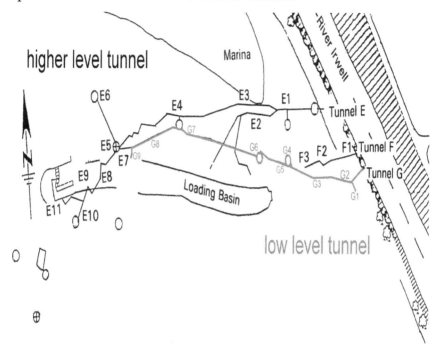

It was immediately apparent that we had been dealing with two quite separate tunnel systems, the distinction being that tunnel E ran at a comparatively high level whilst tunnel G had been driven at a level approximately 5ft lower!

Having connected back to the riverbank, it was now possible to continue the reference system adopted earlier.

The wide mouth from the rear of E4 into tunnel G took on the appearance of a funnel and in hindsight it was now obvious why we had been unable to determine the true shape of the entrance by using probes.

The tunnel really started about 10ft inside the rock face where it could be seen curving strongly to the left and although

entry to the new area of G7 was still difficult due to the very thick silt, we were at least aware of what we would have to deal with over the coming weeks.

As progress was made outbye from G7 it was realised for the third time that movement was only possible with the aid of running water and, more than ever before, the vital role played by the pump was brought to the fore.

Beyond the initial curve it was found that the tunnel was almost perfectly straight until it reached the shaft G6 where it dropped suddenly and then took a double bend, first left and then right[24].

Photo showing Dave Lane at the junction E4/G7.
In the absence of a levelling survey we were forced to assume that the whole of tunnel G had a gradient which dipped towards the riverbank and this led us to

[24] First journey from E5 to G5 was completed by Alan Davies on 21 August 1991

believe that by continuing to remove the silt from the area beyond G5 we would create a better drainage channel.

Working to plan we travelled inwards from the river bank along tunnel G and enjoyed success as the water level dropped in relation to each spade of silt removed.

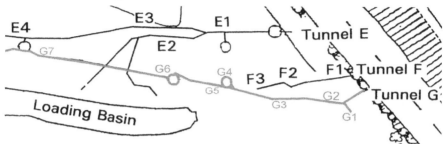

By the time we were in sight of G7 the level had dropped considerably and in doing so revealed an inscription, HB 65, on the right hand wall of the tunnel[25].

Excitement was restrained because although the lettering was similar to the style used in the 18th century, the artist had failed to prefix the year by the century making it impossible for us to calculate an accurate date.

From the depth of the silt at this point we assumed that it would be safe to discount 1965 as a possibility and this gave us at worst 1865, a time which coincided with expansion and redevelopment at Wet Earth.

---

[25] Inscription discovered on 31 August 1991

Chapter 9 – Surface Work

In spite of tight budgets the Greater Manchester Archaeological Unit continued to be funded by the far sighted Salford City Council.

Two major commissions were received enabling the unit to remain on site for much of 1990 and into 1991 but unfortunately as work progressed it became more and more obvious that the term 'archaeological unit' was a misnomer.

The measuring, surveying and careful practical work expected of a true archaeologist were substituted by fancy reports and hasty promises.

Admittedly the subject matter would stand rougher handling than a Roman mosaic but all the same, even in industrial archaeology it is vital that true, proper and regular reports are made of each operation or discovery.

Basically the particular unit used at Wet Earth appeared to be no more than a labouring group, a point well worth remembering for the future!

By June 1990 attention had turned to the head of the loading basin where pit waste and a collapsed banking almost completely  obscured the penstock arch.

Heavy equipment was used to remove the infill and within a matter of weeks the stone walls of the basin itself were revealed to be largely intact. The arch was less fortunate, being in such a poor state of repair that it needed to be dismantled and then restored stone by stone.

Demolition was no problem. Rebuilding was another story!

The archway had originally been constructed on a skew and it was necessary to construct a former in order to retain the correct alignment.

To accommodate the skew it was obvious that masons would have had to cut the hand made bricks on site and it was no surprise when, after substituting modern material, the construction team was unable to recreate the original shape.

A second attempt gave a more acceptable finish and to complement the arch it was decided to re-open the penstock tunnel which had been sealed for over 20 years.

Initially it was feared that the tunnel had been filled in prior to the curtain wall being constructed but after removing a few bricks it was clear that in reality the tunnel had been perfectly preserved.

Photograph showing the head of the loading basin and the arch

Photograph showing the curtain wall during demolition phase

Photograph showing the head of the basin and the penstock archway after reconstruction

Photograph showing the inner archway of the penstock.

View into the penstock tunnel showing the extreme left hand bend towards the wheel chamber

Peter Stott at the wheel chamber 'end' of the penstock tunnel

In November 1990 the GMAU commenced the largest project yet undertaken at Wet Earth Colliery, the location and excavation of what was said to be Brindleys wheel chamber.

Wheel chamber in 1960's

Following on from an unsuccessful trial dig heavy equipment was again brought on site and this time enjoying better luck, the GMAU was able to locate brickwork around the top of the wheel chamber.

The outer walls were discovered some 14ft lower than present ground level.

With pit waste making up the majority of the infill the JCB excavator worked through unknown territory to reveal several features that had not been expected.

Within a relatively short period of time the chamber had been excavated to a depth of almost 30ft but even at this depth there was no sign of a solid floor.

Of the features around the chamber, most obvious was the fact that a huge trough covered the north wall around the penstock outlet. The base of the trough comprised a large grille which appeared to filter water before it passed into the wheel chamber.

Jack Ashworth standing inside wheel chamber during the excavation

A deep void could be seen through the grille but access to this was prevented by large timber beams which continued downwards in a framework extending from the trough itself.

Assuming that Banks & Schofield had correctly interpreted the chamber before it was backfilled, theory dictated that we were looking at the

tailrace inlet. Curiosity however demanded that the timbers were removed for a full inspection.

The timber beams had been slotted and then bolted into the framework in such a manner that they were not to be removed without a major operation being involved.

Certainly they would never be removed whilst the chamber was in use and consequently it was felt that they could not be related to the tailrace.

As the penstock outlet had been sealed with similar timbers it was felt safe to conclude that both sets were placed at the same time, possibly when the water wheel was made redundant.

Comparing the current data with historical information we could see that Banks & Schofield had taken what we now knew to be fixed timbers, to be a sliding sluice gate leading to the tailrace tunnel.

The assumptions had then been stated as 'fact' [26].

Additionally it had long been assumed that the gates, if any, had been controlled by a hinged arrangement however it was now possible to see that some sort of pulley arrangement had been in operation across the penstock, the wheels still visible on the north wall of the chamber.

Without making any realistic enquiries the GMAU had expected to excavate a chamber some 27ft by 20ft by 27ft deep therefore it was no surprise when after reaching a depth of 29ft they declared the job complete and made a request to grade the remaining infill and seal the floor at that level.

Without a doubt the scale of operation had proved far greater than provided for by the GMAU and fortuitously, in February 1991, funds ran short forcing work to cease forthwith.

The new financial year brought more funding and along came the unit with a brochure detailing finalised plans for grading the 'base' and restoring the brickwork around the chamber.

Incredibly the unit management had totally ignored the fact that they had not yet located a solid floor and at project team meetings they had even stated that locating the floor was not essential to interpretation of the chamber.

[26] Banks AG and RB Schofield, Brindley at Wet Earth Colliery, note 9, 89-93

The very depth they had already attained should have indicated that they had excavated far below rock level and this coupled with the fact that loose spoil was still being removed should have led to the conclusion that the spoil was merely infill on top of a solid base.

More ludicrous than anything else was the fact that the unit wanted the City of Salford to pay for an excavation which still had to reveal the one thing of any importance, the tailrace!

Getting nowhere in official circles it was decided that WECEG would carry on the investigation alone and hopefully prove that a solid floor existed.

With such proof it would be possible to demand that the unit fulfil contractual obligations and completely excavate the chamber thus revealing the tailrace inlet.

Dropping into the trough which was by far the lowest point of the area (and the softest digging) it was decided to go down a couple of feet and then probe with a ranging pole.

Working to plan the whole trough was covered and after a mere 20 minutes we had data which revealed a solid base across the test area[27].

Additionally we had located a point at which the metal trough reached bedrock.

Cramped conditions inside the trough prevented the spoil from being removed easily and it was eventually decided that a further attempt would be made to locate the tailrace from inside the tunnel system.

Other features were noted inside the chamber including a circular scour that had already been described by Banks & Schofield.

It had been said that the scour had been gouged by the original water wheel but previously only a section of the circle had been visible and its diameter had not been accurately calculated.

With the infill removed it was possible to examine the whole of the scour but once again our interpretation of the facts gave rise to a different conclusion from that expected.

---

[27] Taking the pulley blocks at the top of the north wall as a base, the depth of the chamber was estimated at 33 ft

Until recently a drawing by Hills and Mullineux[28] had been accepted as the end product of an accurate survey but it was now possible to see that even a fact as basic as the positioning of the axle had been incorrectly plotted.

SECTION THROUGH WHEEL CHAMBER

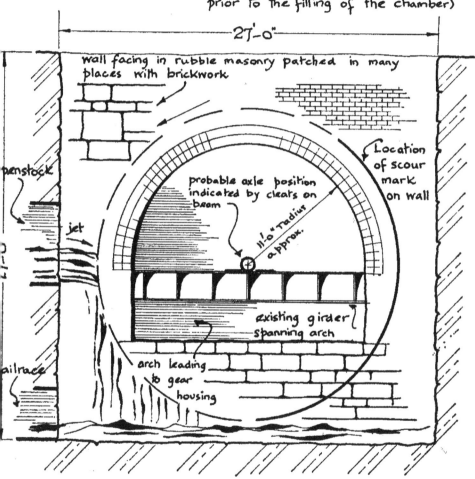

(based on a drawing by Messrs. J. Hills & C. Mullineux made prior to the filling of the chamber)

27'-0"

wall facing in rubble masonry patched in many places with brickwork

penstock

jet

probable axle position indicated by cleats on beam

11'-0" radius approx.

Location of scour mark on wall

existing girder spanning arch

arch leading to gear housing

tailrace

outline shows deduced approximate size of Brindley's original water wheel.

SCALE (FEET)

0   5   10

Fig. 16

[28] Banks AG and RB Schofield, note 9, 90

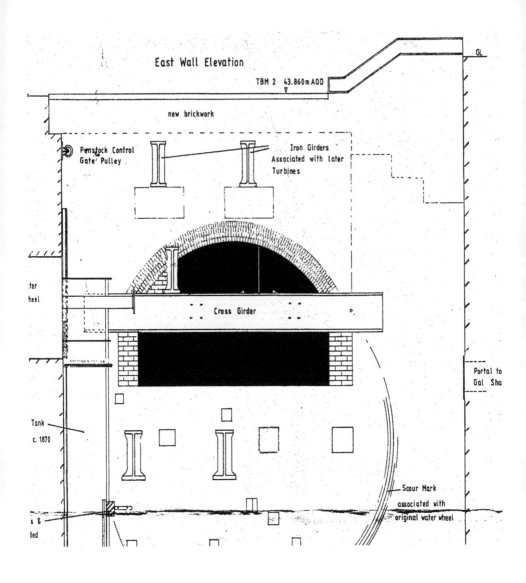

East Wall Elevation

TBM 2 43.860m AOD

GL

new brickwork

Penstock Control
Gate Pulley

Iron Girders
Associated with later
Turbines

ter
heel

Cross Girder

Portal to
Gal Sha

Tank
c. 1870

Scour Mark
associated with
original water wheel

s &
ied

Derek Nicholls drawing of the wheel chamber in 1995

Chapter 10 – Inspection of the Gal Pit & Wheel Chamber Link

On 15 October 1991 the GMAU reported that they had discovered a small conduit leading out of the wheel chamber.

With visions and hopes of this being the tailrace, a site meeting was immediately convened.

Unfortunately the site inspection revealed that the conduit had been driven high in the southern wall of the chamber rather than low on the northern wall.

The conduit had been revealed whilst damaged brickwork was removed prior to restoration and already it had been partly sealed with new brickwork.

After removing the few remaining bricks it was obvious that the conduit actually linked to the gal pit thus allowing entry to the shaft[29].

A cursory glance inside confirmed this fact but a small deposit of infill material prevented comfortable inspection.

[29] Alan Davies & Mark Wright 15 October 1991

Initial disappointment gave way to frantic excitement at the thought of being able to view the potentially intact gal pit.

Eager to examine the conduit more closely we removed the infill and revealed the dimensions to be some 22 inches wide, 32 inches high and 8ft long.

Although the floor appeared to be picked rock, the rest of the conduit was lined with small narrow bricks that could be contemporary with the sinking of the wheel chamber if not the shaft itself.

Less than 15ft above head height we could see the capping fitted by Salford City Council and it was realised that the gal pit was actually far wider than the capping suggested on the surface[30].

Whilst examining the gal pit for signs of an inset it was noticed that the lining had collapsed part way down and also that the walls had bulged in various places.

---

[30] From previous page the visible cap is a 'token' representing the shaft below. The true capping is some 12ft below ground level.   The photos on this page show (top) inset or opening into gal pit (bottom) conduit from wheel chamber to gal pit

Leaning further over the lip it was possible to see that the gal pit was indeed filled with water but we were unable to make proper estimate of the distance due to poor lighting.

At water level we could see what appeared to be a passage driven below the far wall and in the hope that this was an open roadway it was decided to arrange for specialists to descend the gal pit at a future date.

Spurred on by the fact that access to the conduit could be revoked at any time a carefully prepared group set off on 19th October 1991.

Carrying gas detection equipment, breathing apparatus and various caving tackle the intention was to appraise the safety aspect and then make a descent of the shaft.

After rigging suitably belayed safety line we were able to reach out and lower a miners flame safety lamp into the depths.

With the lamp burning brightly as it disappeared into the gloom our fears of gas were somewhat relieved.

At about 75ft from the portal though, the flame was extinguished and with it went our hopes of a safe descent.

A further 50ft remained to water level so, having marked the line at danger point, we prepared to make a second test.

Initially the lamp had been spinning and it was suspected that this had probably contributed to the flame dying out.
Even with this problem corrected, when the mark was reached the flame went out thus confirming the presence of an oxygen deficient atmosphere.

Accepting that a full descent would be dangerous even when wearing breathing apparatus it was decided to leave a 20 ft safety margin and examine the first 50ft of shaft.

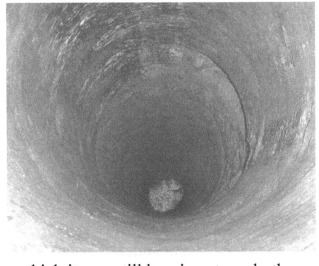

Within a short period of time and making good use of scaffolding inside the wheel chamber, the belays required for abseiling were correctly positioned. The lamp had been lowered to a point at which it was still burning strongly thus giving a clear indication of the maximum depth that could be negotiated with safety.

Final checks of personal safety equipment and of the rope itself were made prior to backing along the conduit to the lip of the shaft and after taking the strain our intrepid explorer[31] disappeared into the void to begin his foot by foot commentary.

Large holes were sighted at various points around the Gal Pit and it was assumed that these would have held timbers during the construction stage or possibly a brattice to divide the shaft into two separate sections.

No ill effects were experienced during the cautious descent and as expected the shaft lining was in poor condition having completely collapsed less than 30ft below the portal.

From here it was possible to see the water level quite clearly however the loose shale and mud that had been exposed behind the brickwork did not inspire confidence and at this point it was decided to abandon the descent.

Ascending the shaft was as much a task as descending although the hardest part appeared to be the final climb back into the conduit.

Once inside the wheel chamber there was a sigh of relief and much laughter which successfully broke up the seriousness of the situation.

---

[31] Perry Westlake on the descent with Russell Williams as anchor man, founder members of the Bury based Underground Exploration Group

It was unfortunate that gas had been present but it was an obstacle that had been expected and catered for and in itself this showed that, properly equipped, the exploration of abandoned shafts was not an impossibility.

The need for co-operation between specialist groups was highlighted during this exercise and many thanks are due to both Perry and Russ who set up and completed the climb on our behalf. It was concluded that the conduit was a tremendous find in its own right and judging from the brickwork across its mouth it had been sealed for many years before the closure of Wet Earth Colliery.

Almost certainly this was the original discharge point through which the water was pumped from the workings, a fact confirmed by the absence of any other break in the gal pit lining.

As the conduit was the only breach in the lining we had certainly disproved Banks and Schofields theory that pump rods and pipework went into the gal pit from the hall adjacent to the wheel chamber.

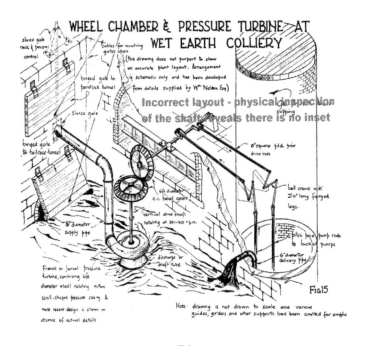

Fig15

74

<u>Chapter 11 - Ventilation Shafts & Underground Canals</u>

Excitement generated by work around the Gal Pit and the fact that the underground survey was getting closer to the central colliery area led to thoughts becoming more diversified.

Had the other shafts been filled or were they open like the Gal Pit? How had the drift mine been sealed? Could we find the supposed underground canal?

Taking advantage of the extra manpower offered by the Bury based, Underground Exploration Group, we decided to make an examination of the ventilation shaft which served the drift mine upto its closure in 1910.

It was hoped that the shaft would be open below its capping thus allowing us to lower a camera for a visual inspection of the roadway and, although a previous attempt had failed to make any progress, a team of nine assembled on 10 October 1991.

As expected the capping proved to be quite substantial and we were forced to dig a trench downwards following the shaft wall.

The capping itself was concrete and appeared to sit on a brick raft which surrounded the true lining. The outer layers of brickwork were fairly easy to remove but when the third and then fourth layers were reached we seemed to be running out of shaft as well as strength.

At last a reverberating echo confirmed the lack of infill and encouraged us to continue.

Eventually the lining succumbed and through the small gap it was possible to see that the shaft wall had been perfectly preserved. A mixture of brick types gave a multicoloured and decorative effect which seemed quite out of place when compared to the gal pit lining.

Stones thrown into the void revealed a solid base which in theory should have been 90ft below surface level, close to where the furnace once stood.

Unfortunately a plumb line proved the depth to be only 75ft and to make matters worse, testing with a flame safety lamp indicated that a serious oxygen deficiency was present at entry level. Several consecutive tests confirmed the position and even with breathing apparatus to hand it was decided that a full inspection would be impossible.

With another question crossed off our list we pushed forward and in an attempt to find more information a visit was made to the British Coal Abandoned Mines section at Staffordshire House where we hoped to examine the various abandonment plans which related to Wet Earth.

Initially it was thought that detailed surface plans would accompany the abandonment plans but it was immediately apparent that the general OS maps were able to provide more precise surface details.

Having worked through 9 sets of documents relating to each of the seams mined, it was almost a chore to open the final parcel which was catalogued as containing 11 plans relating to the Doe Seam.

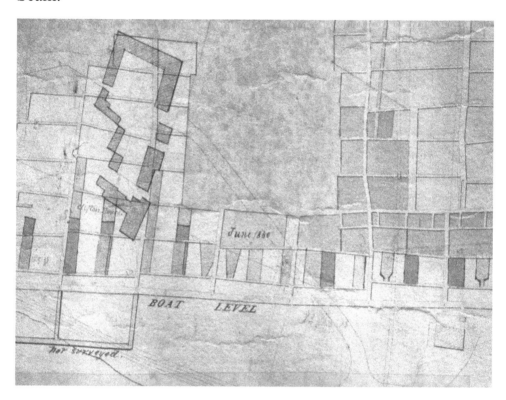

To say that energy flooded back would be an understatement but when the words 'Boat Level' were spotted even a syringe full of adrenalin would have had difficulty in competing.

Dated 1860 the plan was hand coloured to represent different periods of working and finally confirmed the existence of an underground canal at Wet Earth Colliery.
The Old Boat Level was clearly shown as running throughout the Doe Seam some 90 yards below surface level.

Two early shafts known to have been north east of Clifton House Farm are also shown as named pits on the 1860 plan, 'Wet Yard Ladder Pit' and 'Engine Pit', a designation not repeated on any other known plans or even in local lore.

Without doubt we had located the same document that

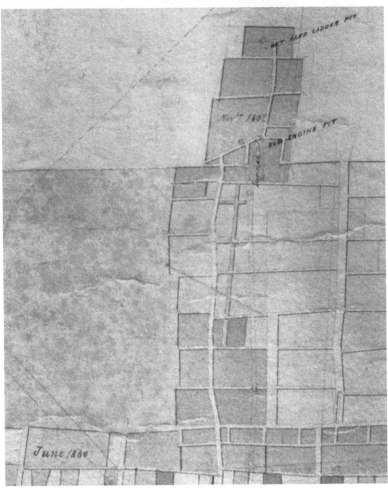

Gaskell[32] had mentioned and to which Charles Hadfield[33] had made reference in 1970.

It would appear that Corbett[34] made the first reference to an underground canal at Wet Earth but he failed to cite the source of his information,

[32] Gaskell, A, The History & Traditions of Clifton, page 34
[33] Hadfield, C and G. Biddle, Canals of NW England vol 2, page 262
[34] Corbett J, note 7 pages 74-75

'the colliery formerly had a canal branch carried for about 8 miles through

its workings, but it has long been out of use'

Hadfield and Biddle at least appear to have sighted the plan even though they failed to make a correct interpretation of what they saw,

'at Wet Earth a plan of the Doe mine workings there dated 1860, shows an

old boat level about 1000 yards long running to the estate boundary, its

probable limit. Its entrance was also that of Brindleys wheelrace'

With the plan unfurled in front of us it was possible to see that a ridiculous mistake had been carried forwards over the years.

Patently the canal existed but unfortunately for all who had put pen to paper, the canal never surfaced and therefore could not be entered via Brindleys wheelrace or any other portal on the hillside.

By failing to double check their sources even respected experts had inadvertently misled their pupils, an error which could had carried on unchecked for many more years.

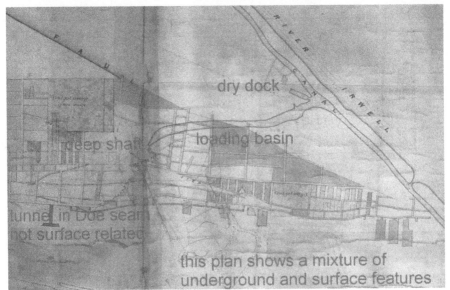

this plan shows a mixture of underground and surface features

Having already discovered more than we hoped for, the other plans were given a cursory glance as we prepared to leave.

The shock on finding a second reference was absolute and we stared in disbelief.

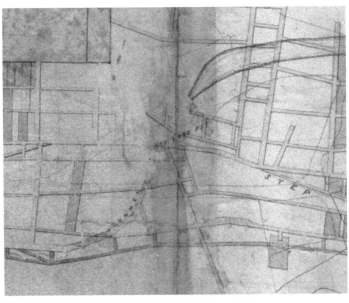

Entitled 'A Plan of the Doe Mine of Clifton Colliery' and dated 1837, the plan was again hand coloured and showed the boat level as a working area extending from the downcast shaft at Wet Earth to beyond the New Pit which we now know as Manor Pit.

In all a distance of about 2,300 yards were covered by the boat level and this appeared to link 3 collieries, Wet Earth, Unity Brook and Manor Pit in a communication network that had not previously been suspected.

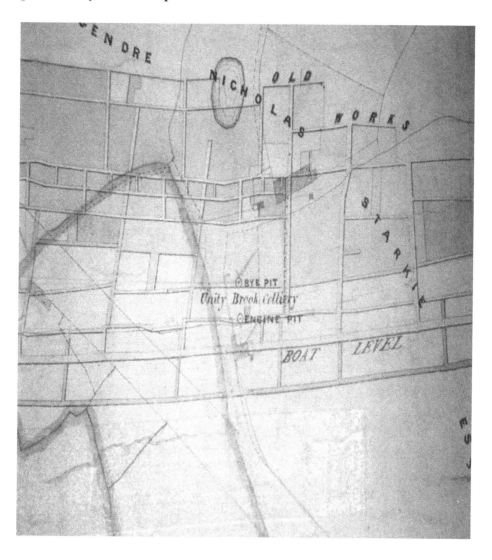

Chapter 12 – Looking for the Tailrace

Realising that we had neglected the rest of the system in favour of making the connection it was a bonus to return to the junction

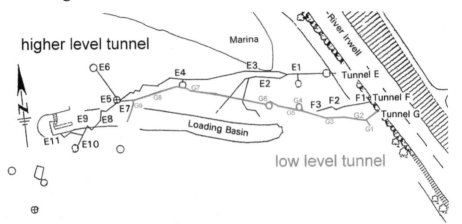

with E7 where we found that the small brick lined tunnel now logged as G9 had drained considerably.

Although even now it was possible to gain entry, it was clear that if the remaining high spots were removed from the connecting tunnelG8, the water would drain more efficiently from the visible 30ft of G9.

Access was not pleasant by any means but it did not prevent us from travelling quickly through the fluid ochre solution.

The narrow, lined tunnel curved gently to the right and within a few feet the entrance had disappeared from sight.

The lining appeared to continue for some distance but with the bulk of our dry suits causing the water to rise we had to return to the junction.

Over the following week the channel created by our movement reduced the water level by a further six inches, a tremendous difference which meant that we were now able to move without displacement becoming a problem.

For almost a year now protective dry-suits had been an absolute necessity, a need further confirmed by the numbing water now encountered along G9.

As the lined section ended we entered a roughly hewn area similar to the section of passage between E5 and E11.

Spectacular but probably unimportant groups of stalactite had formed in various places and these gave an added dimension to what would otherwise have been a very boring and strenuous journey.

Within a relatively short distance, water and roof almost met but as the air seemed fine it was deemed reasonable to continue.

The only way in which forwards motion could be gained was by stretching full length whilst being pushed from the rear.

By successfully using this type of motion a second lined area was reached.

Progress was immediately halted by infill which had choked the passage yet feeling somewhat elated we travelled back secure in the knowledge that we had reached the wheel chamber.

It was not until several days later that a simple measuring tape confirmed how wrong we really were!

The cramped and exhausting conditions below ground made it difficult to gauge linear distance as well as direction and in this case we had misjudged the distance travelled by at least 80 yards.

With drainage improving weekly it was not long before we had unrestricted access to the tunnel and work began at removing the blockage.

Closer examination revealed the outline of a shaft, G11, the

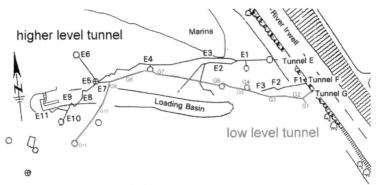

presence of which was confirmed when a small amount of infill was removed.

Large timbers formed a framework which had been surrounded by concrete rubble, bricks and a covering of soil. It appeared that almost by chance the timbers had fallen across the tunnel mouth thus preventing smaller items from making a complete seal.

In one respect this had been a godsend because at least we knew that we had reached a shaft and therefore had a slim chance of  finding that the tunnel continued ahead.

A worrying problem was that water appeared to be exiting the blockage under pressure and unfortunately this could be attributed to more than one reason.

At best we could hope that the spray was caused by water seeping down from rock level but at worst we could find that the tunnel ahead was flooded and the seepage was due to a massive build up of pressure.

Finding a tunnel flooded in those circumstances would be little different from opening up a high pressure hydrant in an enclosed space and without doubt the consequence would be horrendous.

After removing a quantity of bricks and timber the shaft was more clearly defined but by now the blockage had been undermined to such an extent that further progress would again prove dangerous.

One plus factor was that the water had not increased in either strength or volume and this alleviated the fear of sudden flooding. Exercising caution it was decided that because much of the remaining infill was a mixture of bricks and soil it would probably be worth blasting water into the obstruction.

This would hopefully wash out soft materials and eventually force its way through any gaps to reveal the shaft lining or, more importantly, the long hidden blackness of a tunnel mouth.

Our survey had plotted G11 slightly to the south east of the wheel chamber at a point which corresponded with the position

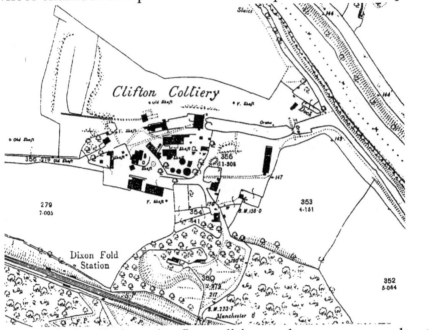

of a shaft detailed on the first edition ordnance survey sheet.

To reach the wheel chamber from here a tunnel would have to be driven north west, almost in fact at 90 degrees to the entry tunnel.

Even after allowing for such a drastic change in direction, the tunnel would most likely hit the eastern wall of the wheel chamber unless it was driven well below the depth of the chamber itself to be fed by a drop shaft near the north wall.

As expected the powerful jet of water was able to penetrate the blockage however the sound of rushing water and an immediate increase in volume suggested that a hasty retreat would be in order.

The thick sludge did not lend itself to any form of quick movement but even so it did not take long to travel the length of unlined passage.

Standing exhausted it was obvious that the noise and volume was constant rather than increasing and after a few minutes contemplation it was decided to return to the choke.

The noise by now was tremendous but still the source could not be traced.

Pulling at the loose rubble resulted in a larger flow and it was soon obvious that the water was coming from behind and to the right of the remaining infill. Bridge rail and timbers were removed, the flow increasing all the time, and eventually the water began to open its own channel.

The torrent pushed loose bricks and pit spoil out of the way and finally it was there.

A tunnel stretching away into the distance[35]

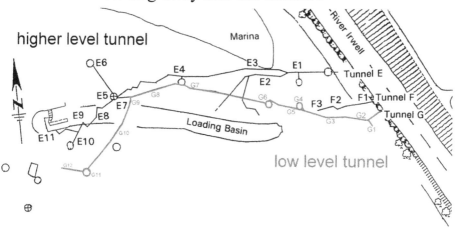

With the opening less than 1ft square it was difficult to see anything other than the fact that the tunnel, G12, was brick

---

[35] Mark Wright 9 November 1991

lined, water filled to within 6 inches of the roof and heading in the right direction.

It seemed too good to be true but all the same there could be no denying that the tunnel was there and awaiting investigation.

Chapter 13 – Shocks & New Discoveries

Concentrating on the weak right hand side of the choke it was not long before a sizeable gap had been opened[36].

Large blocks were the only remaining obstacle but even these came free and, along with other infill, were used to create a retaining wall.

Once the loose material had been

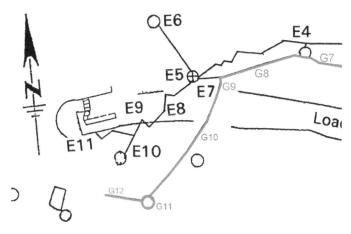

consolidated it was possible to pass beyond the shaft, a somewhat un-nerving experience as we could not be certain if the suspended rubble was quite as secure as it appeared to be.

An ochre bank lay ahead however it was so fluid that the slightest touch caused it to flow outwards.

As we pushed on, our unceremonious floundering proved to be more than 'the slightest touch' and the bank literally shivered and then emptied out of the tunnel.

---

[36] Perry Westlake, Alan Davies & Mark Wright 13 November 1991

Thousands of gallons of slurry must have pushed out causing the level to rise as far back as the junction with E7/G8.

Moving rapidly now we approached what appeared to be a dead end however a strong cold flow was felt coming from 90 degrees to the main section of tunnel and, on investigating, a small portal was discovered, G13.

Barely visible the opening was about 15 inches wide but less than 8 inches high. Peering inside we were dumbfounded.

The narrow beam of our lamps highlighted a large unlined cavern with a coal seam visible in the strata. Needless to say, as excitement grew stronger, it did not take much  encouragement to grab the sides of the portal and slither through the gap.

Water filled nose and ears and whilst scrabbling around for support the flow increased considerably bringing with it a more solid ochre  deposit. The increase momentarily blocked the portal but when it subsided the opening had been flushed clear allowing the duck to be avoided.

The floor of the cavern appeared to be some 3ft higher than the tunnel we had left and from this raised position it was obvious that another passage headed back over the top of G12/G13.

Proving less substantial than expected, a mixture of shale and silt was swept aside from the higher tunnel allowing us to move forwards. Unfortunately a loose mixture of bricks and rubble ended our progress within 40ft.

Close examination revealed that the infill was actually at the base of a shaft and although the blockage was formidable it looked as if it would be possible to 'worm-hole' around the loose material near the side walls.

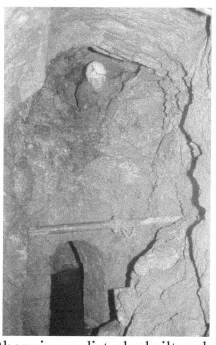

Less than an hours digging revealed that the tunnel really did continue but more importantly it gave access to an area that had obviously been travelled recently.

Scrape marks were visible in the otherwise undisturbed silt and as we crawled through the rubble, it was apparent that we had linked with E10, the gas house passage that we had thought to be impenetrable.

Having accepted that the cavern was actually a continuation of tunnel E, an

immediate examination of the coal seam revealed an anomalous deposit of fireclay, E12, which appeared to be a deliberate stopping at the entrance to yet another tunnel.

Initially it was felt that this could be the way into early workings that had followed the dip of the seam however as the fireclay was carefully removed we discovered that although a tunnel had been sealed, it merely led to a blind or partly filled chamber.

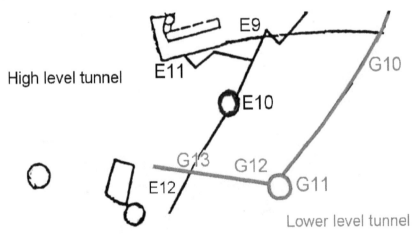

Standing in the 'cavern' we could see the main section of tunnel becoming lined and curving away out of sight.

Progress was steady and we quickly reached a junction, E13.
Rubble prevented us from going ahead but we had a clear run
into the left hand
branch from which
the greater part of
the water was
exiting.

Travelling slightly
uphill we followed a
strong right hand
bend which brought
us to the source of
our water flow.
Stalactite formations
almost hid the
entrance to a small
shaft, E16, driven
upwards from the
tunnel roof.

Less than 10ft high,
the shaft opened to a

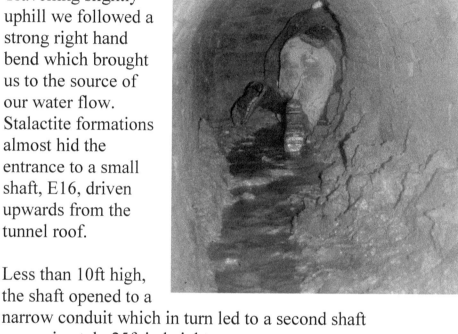

narrow conduit which in turn led to a second shaft
approximately 25ft in height.

A timber bricking ring was visible just above floor level but this
important feature had almost been destroyed by a cascade of
water that had penetrated the capping at surface level. Some 15ft
beyond E16, the tunnel sloped steeply downwards and became
impassable due to a semi-liquid silt that reduced headroom to
about 8 inches.

By squeezing into the gap the tunnel could be seen continuing at 90 degrees to the left but the constriction caused such a claustrophobic feeling that we returned to E12 in order to appraise the situation.

Events over the following three weeks altered the whole Wet Earth concept and threw a different light onto our previous discoveries.

Travelling to G13 via the gas house tunnel we were again put in the embarrassing position of staring dumbfounded at new tunnels that had been revealed by the receding water

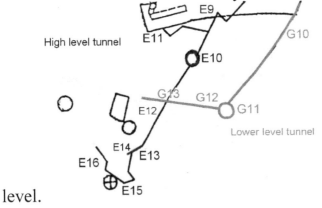

level.

Where we had assumed a dead end, the tunnel could be seen continuing into the distance albeit at a much reduced size.

To make matters worse a side branch could be seen running off at about 45 degrees to the main section and this too had the appearance of continuing for some distance.

Both passages were only just visible but as work continued we dropped the level by a further 6 inches providing just enough airspace to justify an attempt at traversing the side branch, G14.

Movement inside the conduit was restricted by the thickening silt and a number of large timbers that had become wedged against the walls.

Whilst clearing a channel along this section a childs clog [37] was discovered and at present this important artifact is awaiting freeze drying at Bolton Museum.

The conduit ended in a chamber, G15, roughly 12ft by 12ft and about 7ft high. Three walls were constructed in brick however the fourth wall, directly opposite

the conduit comprised large stone blocks similar to those in the loading basin and the wheel chamber.

A further two openings were cut into this wall but unfortunately both were filled within a few feet.

The infill was made up of brickwork and pit waste, a mixture that easily came away to extend the right hand opening by about 3ft.

---

[37]Mark Wright 20 November 1991

Spurred on by a change in the quality of air and a sudden lowering of the temperature, it was no less of a surprise when the soft waste gave way to an inky black void[38].

A framework of scaffolding immediately revealed that we had broken through to the wheel chamber although from our horizontal position it was impossible to say exactly where we were!

The elation at connecting with the wheel chamber was tremendous.

---

[38] Mark Wright, Alan Davies, Perry Westlake & Matthew Smith 23 November 1991

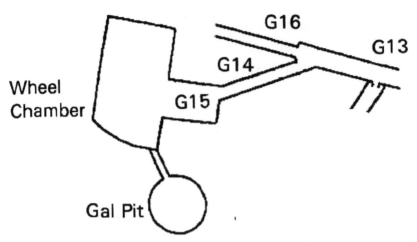

We scrabbled through the newly enlarged opening totally oblivious of the sub zero temperature that quickly replaced the warm, humid air in which we had been working below ground.

The realisation that we had emerged from the eastern wall of the wheel chamber rather than the northern wall confirmed the suspicions that had been voiced earlier.

It was now clear that the tailrace inlet had been constructed slightly below and to either side of the water wheel, a fact highlighted by the position of the scour mark.

The chamber G15 was obviously a catchment area. Its existence, however had not been expected and appeared to be something of a luxury.

The same thing could be said for everything about the tailrace.

Why such large tunnels when the pumps themselves were not capable of removing comparably large quantities of mine water? Why the unusually indirect route to the river?

Why? Why? Why?

Although tracing the tailrace had been our primary objective we found that success brought with it many more questions.

On the face of it the tailrace did not appear to be directly below the penstock. We had proved tradition wrong and highlighted the dangers of 'assuming' rather than obtaining physical evidence.

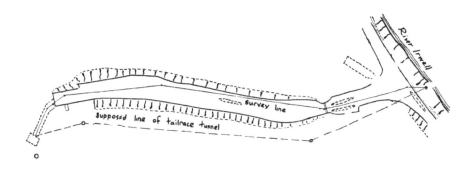

Returning to the junction of G13/G14 we pushed on, entering G16, the lower section of tunnel[39]. Conditions were difficult with less than 8 inches between water and roof however it was possible to push the slurry to one side and quickly move into the gap caused by displacement.

The whole procedure was exhausting and claustrophobic but it worked and after some 30ft we found that the tunnel abruptly changed direction.
The brick lining had disappeared being replaced by stone blocks similar to those in the wheel chamber and it appeared that infill had sealed what could be a continuation at 90 degrees to the left.

It was felt that this could be a second link to the wheel chamber, almost certainly to the northern wall and very possibly to the trough.

---

[39] Mark Wright 30 November 1991

Moving away from the blockage proved more difficult than expected due to the fact that the water level had somehow risen and was continuing to rise.

It was still possible to displace the slurry but helmet and lamp had to be removed to compensate for the reduced headroom.

Some 12 ft back towards the junction a break was discovered in the lining on the northern side of the tunnel and flowing out of it was the coldest water yet encountered on the system.

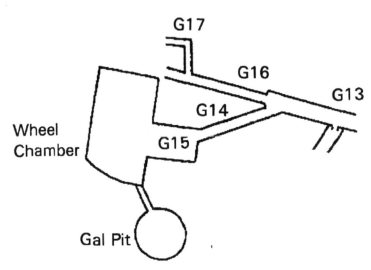

Heavy chunks of ochre were floating near the break and it appeared that by cutting a channel inbye, a plug had been released at the entrance to a side tunnel, G17.

Finding another entrance seemed almost laughable!

Over a period of ten days we had made more discoveries that we had made over the last 18 months and now, looking into the 18 inch mouthing it appeared that we had not yet finished by any means.

Realising that the water level had stabilised and more than eager to continue a successful day it was deemed safe to brave the 4 inch headroom and enter the side tunnel.

Struggling with only nose and eyes above the ochry water it took an age to complete the 8 ft after which headroom fortunately improved.

Turning at 90 degrees to the left the tunnel increased to about 30 inches diameter and continued beyond the range of an Oldham lamp.

The silt was similar in consistency to that which had been encountered when G11 was breached and as it filled the tunnel for an unknown distance it was felt an opportune moment had arisen to return to the main group near G13.

The importance of G16 and G17 could not be disputed.

On one hand it was possible that G16 was the original tailrace with the G14/15 link being a later modification, whilst on the other hand G17 potentially took us beyond what was considered to be the Brindley system.

Again it was felt that this could be a modification making use of the established drainage conduits and having decided to make a full examination at the earliest opportunity, we returned to the new section within a few days[40].

The water level along G16 had dropped a few inches boosting morale and enabling us to make easy penetration of G17 where we found that the silt was indeed similar to that encountered at the choke, G11.

---

[40] Perry Westlake & Mark Wright, 2 December 1991

Safety conscious we agreed to keep a distance between each other in case help had to be summoned and as expected, even with just one man moving forwards, the silt began to flow outbye at a tremendous rate.

Before 25 ft had been covered the whole tunnel appeared to be in motion.

A retreat merely increased the speed of the flow and before G16 was in sight, panic had set in.

The whole tunnel was sumping and it was obvious that the remaining 20ft would have to be travelled underwater or we faced the possibility of drowning in the flooded passage.

The realisation and the submersion were pretty well simultaneous and proved more a case of instinct that conscious intent.

Water hardly described the vile substance which filed every orifice and it was fortunate that by now the surge had increased to such an extent that only a few seconds passed before emerging like a cork from a bottle.

It was quite unnerving to look back and see that both G14 and G16 had disappeared and it was with some relief that we passed through G13 into the higher levels of tunnel E.

The cold clean water along this

section facilitated a quick wash and it was only a little while before we were able to drop back down and inspect the damage.

The flow had stopped and amazingly the level had returned to its original height allowing us to pass back towards G17.

Quickly reaching the 90 degree turn it was a surprise to see that less than 8 inches of silt now covered what was obviously a brick floor. The tunnel appeared to be climbing slightly, a feature which became more apparent as we carefully moved forwards.

Following a strong left hand bend we reached a junction where a passage of some 42 inch diameter cut across to the left, G18 and the right, G19.

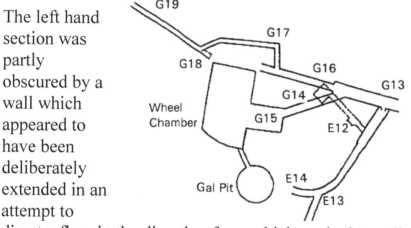

The left hand section was partly obscured by a wall which appeared to have been deliberately extended in an attempt to direct a flow in the direction from which we had travelled.

A second wall sealed this section less than 10ft from the junction.

To our right the passage continued for some distance however the silt began to deepen and we were forced to probe it with a rake in the hope that its movement could be controlled.

So far into the system we obviously wanted to avoid a repetition of the earlier surge and when the flow looked in danger of getting out of hand we decided to retreat.

Using our bulky suits to keep the silt behind us we reached G16 and within a short time had ascended the wheel chamber to surface level.

Tracing our route above ground we appeared to have circled around the wheel chamber itself and were heading across the site roughly between the upcast and downcast shafts.

This was an interesting point because all along we had worked on the assumption that ochry water was a result of mine drainage and, as we were still heading into large volumes of ochre, it seemed reasonable to assume that even now we were travelling a drainage conduit possibly of equal importance to the tailrace.

Hoping to confirm our theory we returned two days later and although we found that the silt level had dropped, fresh staining indicated that G16 had sumped since our last visit.

This caused us to adopt precautions similar to those used previously and accordingly we left a back up man at the entrance to G17.

It appeared that each time we disturbed an area of silt, a chain reaction liquefied other, as yet undisturbed areas. To some extent this had worked in our favour and we were able to push further along G19 without meeting any problems[41].

Climbing more obviously than before the brick lining eventually gave way to sandstone and we passed into a slightly enlarged area, G20.

A much taller brick lined tunnel continued ahead, G21, while a shaft had been driven upwards, G22.

A large pipe terminated part way up the shaft whilst timber, bridge rail and brickwork splayed out from its base effectively forming a 3ft high dam across the entrance to G21.

Realising that the dam was unstable it was not possible to do anything more than glance up the shaft before turning back.

A sudden roar and blast of air dispelled any thoughts of lingering and, part running, crawling and even swimming, the lengths of G19, G17 and G16 were safely negotiated.

As the tunnel quietly sumped we realised that one of our team was absent.

As quickly as it had risen the water fell and somewhat worried we moved towards G17 where ochre still dripped from the roof.

Seemingly endless a further increase in flow was followed by a tremendous splash and out of the mud appeared our missing mate[42].

---

[41] Perry Westlake & Alan Davies, 4 December 1991
[42] Perry Westlake

Having deliberately released the dam he discovered that G21 was of interest although blocked after some 25ft and had then

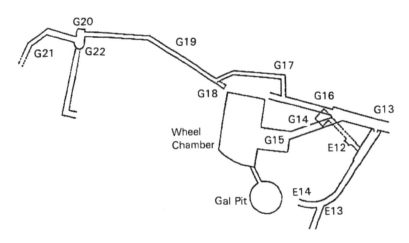

waited on high ground until conditions allowed an easy exit.

Although unorthodox in timing and method, breaching the dam negated a danger that would have had to be faced before our exploration could continue.

On returning to G19 some days later we discovered that the flow had been forceful enough to flush the tunnel almost clear of silt and, working without fear of being trapped we separated hoping to clear the blockages from G21 and G22[43].

Within a little while we were able to stand inside the shaft itself where an examination of the pipe revealed that not only did it continue upwards, it also ran into a small conduit, G23, that had been driven through the lining some 10ft above floor level[44].

---

[43] Alan Davies, Perry Westlake & Mark Wright, 14 December 1991
[44] Mark Wright & Alan Davies

Once again our earlier assumption had been confirmed.

Almost certainly we had been working in material pumped out of the deep seams, a fact which stood as clear testament to the reliability of a scheme that had been completed some 60 years prior to the downcast being sunk.

Similar in size to the Gal Pit/Wheel Chamber link, access to the conduit was initially difficult due to a metal plate that had become wedged part way across the entrance and even when entry had eventually been gained, we found that movement was further restricted by the pipe which had been centrally positioned on timber supports.

Having travelled a distance of only 60ft we turned 90 degrees to the left and halted on the edge of a huge void.

Moving the lamp beam from side to side it was immediately obvious that the void was in fact a shaft which, unlike the Gal Pit was approximately 17ft diameter and furnished with many fittings.

Guide wires, communication cables, water pipes and a variety of other appendages could be seen all around but more importantly than anything else we could see a box, a striking feature that we knew had already been described by James Robinson who worked at Wet Earth Colliery from 1914[45].

Unbelievably we had located the downcast shaft at Wet Earth Colliery and beyond our wildest hopes it was still open[46].

[45] SMM, Robinson notes and photograph
[46] Perry Westlake, 14 December 1991

WET EARTH COLLIERY SCRAPBOOK.

Compiled by Dave Lane.

Introduction.

For many years I have waited for someone to write a book about the colliery of Wet Earth at Clifton, near Manchester. As no book has so far materialised yet people are always asking for more details about the mine, I have put together this brief collection of articles, information sheets and photographs to satisfy both myself and others who are interested both in the colliery and the general area.

This scrapbook has been produced only for my own interest and will not be "published" in any proper sense of this word, although I may run off a few copies for friends and the odd person who has expressed interest. A copy of it will be placed on the Internet.

The scrapbook is NOT a "book" about Wet Earth. One hopes that such a volume may eventually materialize - authored by someone who knows a lot more than I do about the subject - and who is better at writing! In the meantime, just dip into this publication! Although parts of this book have been written by the compiler, a great deal of material is merely extracts from the work of others. Credit has been given to the writers if known. Extracts have also been taken from the Information boards which used to exist all around the site (but which have been repeatedly vandalised and now no longer exist) and also from some information sheets I have come across. If anyone recognizes "their" writings, just let me know and I'll credit you for your text immediately!

My thanks for the bulk of the information and pictures in this publication are directed entirely to all members of the Wet Earth Exploration Group who have collected and supplied much the information contained here. Special thanks are due to Alan Davies, the last curator of the sadly lamented Lancashire Mining Museum, who took many of the photos in this scrapbook. Thanks to all!

Although some years ago, the underground tunnels of Wet Earth Colliery were available for all to see via the conducted tours given by the Exploration Group, there is now no longer access by anyone! For a variety of highly spurious and doubtful reasons, entrance to all the underground workings has now been forbidden both by the Coal Authority and Salford Council. One hopes that sanity will one day prevail and that local people will once again be able to visit and look at their historical heritage underground at Wet Earth Colliery. In the meantime you're stuck with just this scrapbook!

A brief overview of Wet Earth Colliery.

Wet Earth Colliery is located at Clifton, on the southern bank of the River Irwell near Manchester. Coal has been mined in this area for centuries but one of the first major pits was that at Wet Earth, perhaps earlier known as Wet Yard Pit. We believe that the first major shaft to be sunk was the Gal Pit but this proved problematic, with large amounts of water entering the mine. James Brindley was brought in to try to solve the water problem.

He designed and built a system to help drain the mines, bringing water from the Irwell, via a weir some distance upstream. An underground tunnel conveyed the water under fields at Ringley and under the River Irwell through an inverted siphon which in turn fed the water to an underground water wheel which operated the mine pumps. The water both from the water wheel and the mine was passed back to the river by yet more underground tunnels.

The colliery developed over many years changing from a one shaft site, to two deep shafts plus a drift mine. The water pumping system evolved from water wheel, through water turbine and thence to steam power.

The mine closed in 1927.

The service or maintenance tunnel, clearly showing the hand hewn pick marks.

The Geology of the Wet Earth Colliery Area. By E. Todhunter.

Several ages of rock occur in the vicinity of the Wet Earth Colliery in the Irwell valley at Clifton.

Alluvium	<10,000 years ago
Glacial Deposits	10,000 to 2 million
Triassic	190 to 230 million years
Carboniferous (Westphalian)	290 to 315 million years

These rocks were formed under climate conditions varying from tropical swamps to hot arid deserts and the intense cold of the Ice Age.

Carboniferous.

The oldest rocks of the Carboniferous period represent a time, 290 to 315 million years ago, when Britain was just north of the equator and had a hot, humid, tropical climate. A large part of Britain, including Lancashire, was low lying tropical swamps crossed by large meandering rivers. These rivers periodically overflowed and flooded the swamps killing and burying the vegetation and peat in layers of mud and sand.

The sources of the rivers and sediments was high ground to the far north where erosion was taking place. To the south, deltas built out into the open sea. New swamps developed on the sand banks and flood plains, until these too were buried by floods of sediments as the rivers repeatedly burst their banks and changed course. As the many layers of swamp vegetation, mud and sand were buried by more and more sediments, they have been compressed, the water squeezed out and consolidated into layers of rock:

Vegetation and peat	became	coal
Soil	became	seatearth and fireclay
Mud and Clay	became	mudstone and shale
Silt	became	siltstone
Sand	became	sandstone

Vegetation and peat is more spongy and compressable than sand or mud and a 1 metre thick layer or seam of coal is the result of compression of about 10 metres of peat.

Fragments of the swamp vegetation are also preserved in the mudstones and sandstones as fossilized leaves, branches, roots, spores and seeds. Some of the insects, mollusks, crustaceans and amphibians that lived in the swamps, rivers and lagoons were buried in the mud and are now fossils.

These coal bearing rocks of the Westphalian Stage of the Carboniferous Era are commonly termed the Coal Measures. The carbon preserved in the coal seams is a valuable natural energy resource and it has been exploited for hundreds of years in the Lancashire coalfield, which stretches from Oldham to Liverpool and Stockport to Burnley. Clays and sandstones from the Coal Measures have been used for brick making and building stone.

In the Clifton area the Coal Measures are cut by a major NW to SE fault – the Irwell Valley Fault. This fault coincides with the River Irwell Valley and crosses the Irwell at the bend in the river to the north of the marina. The approximate line of the Irwell Valley Fault is marked on the map of the Wet Earth Colliery Trail and can be seen in the Wet Earth adit.

To the SW of the fault the Coal Measures are at the surface, to the NE of the Irwell Valley Fault the Coal Measures have been down faulted by a maximum of 1,00 meters (3,000 feet) and are now beneath the younger Triassic sandstones. West of the fault several coal seams outcrop at the surface or at shallow depths below the glacial deposits. The coal seam outcrops trend approximately WnW to ESE and dip steeply to the S at an inclination of about 1 in 3.5. The coal seams outcropping in the Clifton area are (in decending stratigraphical order):

Rams
Windmill
Black
Doe
Five Quarters
Hell Hole

Clifton was a rich area of the coalfield and many shafts were sunk to mine these coal seams. The Doe coal seam outcrops on the N bank of the River Irwell to the W of the Giants Seat Gorge where a bank of grey
shale occurs containing flakes of coal. This outcrop would have been seen by early miners. The Doe seam in a shaft section at Wet Earth Colliery is 9 foot 7.5 inches thick and was the first seam to be worked when deep mining began in Clifton during the mid 18th century.

Triassic
East of the Irwell Valley Fault the Triassic Sherwood (formally the Bunter) sandstones occur. These rocks are younger (about 210 million years old) than the Carboniferous Westphalian Coal Measure rocks (310 million years old).

The Sherwood Sandstones are well exposed on the banks and floor of the River Irwell downstream from Giant's Seat Gorge and occur at the adit entrances to the Wet Earth Colliery on the Western Bank of the River Irwell. The rocks are weak, porous, mottled reddish-brown, cross-bedded sandstones with well rounded millet seed sand grains and occasionally a few well rounded and sub-angular quartzitic pebbles.

Prior to the deposition of the Triassic rocks great earth movements took place during the Hercynian orogeny (mountain building period). North-south compression and uplift of the Carboniferous rocks occurred with folding and faulting.

The Triassic Sherwood sandstones were deposited in hot arid desert conditions, when Britain lay north of the equator in the Tropics and the mountain chains formed during the Hercynian orogeny were being eroded. Great thicknesses of sediment accumulated in subsiding intermontane basins brought down by flash floods and reworked by wind and water.

The Triassic rocks are stratigraphically above the carboniferous rocks but faulting has moved them to the same level as the Carboniferous rocks in the eastern part of the Wet Earth Colliery separated by the major fault, the Irwell Valley Fault. The main Wet Earth Colliery adit westwards from it's entrance on the banks of the River Irwell passes through Triassic rocks, through the crush zone of the Irwell Valley Fault plane and into the Carboniferous strata.

Glacial Deposits and Aluvium.
During the Pleistocene period (about 1 to 2 million years ago) Lancashire was covered by ice sheets, which melted finally about 10,000 years ago leaving behind glacial till (boulder clay) on the high ground adjacent to the Irwell Valley and spreads of fluvio-glacial sands and gravels in the Irwell Valley.

The youngest deposits are the river alluvium of the Irwell Valley Terraces, still being laid down in times of flood.

General Wet Earth Colliery Information *(Author unknown)*

Wet Earth Colliery and its history would be similar to many of the thousands of other collieries once making up the Lancashire Coalfield but for two aspects.

Firstly, that world famous canal engineer James Brindley (1716-1772) came here in his mid thirties, soon after setting himself up as a consultant wheelwright and millwright, to devise an ingenious water powered pumping system. Secondly, that the colliery operated for over 180 years, from around 1740 until 1928, a very long time compared to an average mine's lifetime.

The name of the colliery probably derives from locally used ones and during its lifetime has been known as Wet Earth Pit, Clifton Colliery and Wet Earth Colliery.

Mining in this area is documented back at least to the 16th century. Many isolated shafts are present amongst the fields. These would have been shallow ladder pits working close to the outcrop of seams such as the Doe which was 9 feet 7 inches thick.

Systematic and efficient methods of coal working became more widespread in the late 17th century. By the early 18th century a number of shafts would have been at work within the Clifton estate especially down to the Doe seam which outcrops near the S bend in the River Irwell to the west.

The shaft adjacent to the wheelchamber reached the Doe seam at a depth of 90 metres, due to its dipping down at 1 in 3.5. As the shaft here was associated with Brindley's waterwheel was the closest to the Irwell Valley Fault on the eastern side of the mining district this was the ideal location for the main water pumping shaft. Water from the workings could gravitate to the sump of this shaft.

The Brindley/Fletcher pumping scheme would be of limited power. This determined the shaft depth. It is said that before the arrival of the waterwheel the workings were drained by winding a kibble (a large iron bucket) into the shaft sump where it filled. This was then raised by a horse gin to the surface and discharged.

It is known that the pumping system was of limited power as a plan of 1860 shows workings to the dip of the underground canal drowned out.

The arrival of the Evans and Pilkingtons seven years later meant an investment of capital and the replacement of the waterwheel with a turbine.

An old plan of the Doe seam shows that as well as the shaft here, a number of other shafts to the west were sunk to the seam, with older working from ladder pits nearer to the outcrop. Also an underground canal was in operation reaching as far as the outskirts of Kearsley, disused by about the 1850's.

Coal extracted could be dragged or tubbed down to the canal and then brought by narrow boat to the shaft inset to be wound up in large baskets of up to 14 hundredweight capacity. A landsale yard on the surface then sold the coal which could either be carried away in baskets and sacks or pack horses would carry large lumps in special frames.

An additional shaft was sunk (amongst the trees on the west side banking) in 1804, with the first Doe coal being wound up on 18th January 1805. Around the late 1860's a ventilation shaft was sunk to complement the new downcast shaft (which fresh air passed down) to a depth of 200 yards where the Trencherbone seam lay. The downcast shaft was later deepened to 285 yards to reach the Sapling seam in the 1890's.

As well as the three shafts in the area, a few yards to the east was the entrance to adrift mine. Further details of the drift are in a later article.

At the turn of the century the colliery was working the Cannel (gas producing coal), Trencherbone, Victoria, Doe, Five Quarters and Crombouke seams. Self acting inclines in the workings delivered coal to the main pony haulage road, with up to 12 at work and stabled near the pit bottom.

A tunnel was driven through the Irwell Valley Fault in 1910 to reach the Worsley Four Foot seam beyond. This district only lasted four years as excessive water was encountered.

After 1917 only the Plodder and Victoria seams were being worked and only the Plodder continued after the 1921 strike. A decision to temporarily close the colliery in February 1928 on economic grounds became the final blow and the colliery never reopened.

A basic tour of the tunnels of Wet Earth.

Around 1989 a number of individuals had started to look at the various
tunnel entrances on the banks of the river Irwell at Clifton, with a view to
opening some of them up for further exploration. At the time, the
entrances were almost completely silted up and entry was not possible in any
meaningful way. By 1990, Alan Davies, the curator of the late Lancashire
Mining Museum, was consulted and within a matter of months, he
brought together a group of enthusiasts and formed the Wet Earth
Exploration Group who were briefed to delve deeper into the fascinating, if
somewhat frustrating, remnants of Wet Earth Colliery.

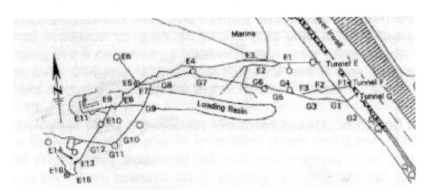

The main tunnels are marked E, & G and are usually referred to as the
"Service" (or "Main" tunnel) and the "Tailrace" tunnel respectively. Also
shown on the plan are the various shafts on each tunnel.

Over the next eight years, much of the silt and debris blocking the tunnels
were removed, all of it being dug out and removed by spade and
wheelbarrow!

There are two major tunnels, the "Tailrace" tunnel and the "Service" tunnel.
The exact purpose of the service tunnel is not known but it may have acted
as an overflow passage for the tailrace tunnel - and it also acts as an exit for
water from the dry dock above.

The Service or Main tunnel.
The entrance is some 8 or 9 feet high and the initial passage remains at this
height (this gives you an idea about how much silt had to be removed!).
The whole tunnel complex is hand hewn in the sandstone and would have
been constructed with only the light from tallow candles.

120

The branch tunnels in the left wall of the service tunnel viewed from the river entrance. Photo by Alan Davies.

Within the first thirty yards, are two tunnels in the left hand wall which were used for drainage purposes, one of them being the drainage tunnel for the dry dock above. At the point where the dry dock water met the main tunnel, hand made nails were washed down from the dock above, and have solidified on the floor to a depth of a foot. A channel to remove standing water from the tunnel had to be cut through this "nail bed" using a pneumatic drill.

Dave Turner using a pneumatic drill to get through the "bed of nails".

The tunnel carries on for another 20 yards then goes up a step and becomes about 6 foot high – although taller people have to bend their heads in places.

The passage is now fairly straight with the roof varying from a pitched design to a flat surface. This section of the tunnel system is totally dry except for times when the River Irwell is in full flood and it fills to the roof with water. It is hard to imagine that this tunnel was being constructed round about the time of the French Revolution at a period when women and children were working as the norm in coal mining ventures.

This whole section of tunnel was hewn by hand, with lighting by tallow candles only. There could well have been women and children involved in its construction.

Dave Lane inspecting one of the many small alcoves in the tunnel walls used for placing candles in the days prior to the advent of electric lighting.
By the way, Dave has lost an AWFUL lot of weight since this photo was taken- the double chin has almost vanished – at least that's what he claims to his wife

After a hundred yards or so, the tunnel changes character considerably, as it nears the Irwell Valley Fault, the strong sandstone giving way to shales which require extra brick support. Only yards before reaching this point, there is an entrance in the left hand wall giving access to the "Square Shaft" with a further tunnel slanting off on the right hand side. The right hand tunnel is still blocked by silt and is unexplored.

The Square shaft is capped at the surface and was probably used in the construction of the tunnels. Rope marks can be seen on the shaft sides. The Square shaft has entrances to both the Service tunnel and to the Tailrace tunnel although the floor of the latter is about 4 feet lower than the Service tunnel floor.

The low section just prior to the bricked up section which passes through the Irwell Valley Fault. Photo shows Alan Davies leading a group of brownies through the tunnels. Alan has to stoop a lot lower than the brownies!

For the time being we'll carry on along the Service tunnel which now lowers considerably and eventually becomes entirely brick lined. You can see a miners initials carved on the wall around this point.

The passage twists and turns as the miners strove to avoid the worst areas of bad rock forming the fault. The photo shows the awkward height and most people breath a sigh of relief when they leave this section. Even after the brick lined section, there is still a fairly low passage which passes through an area of safe yet broken rock.

The section of un-bricked, rough rock as the tunnel passes through the Irwell Valley Fault. The fault is not a clean "fault", but consists of around some 30 feet of "broken rock".

At the end of this short section of passage we come to a junction where four tunnels meet. This area is known as the "Pump Shaft" for the rusting remains of a pump are here with pipes leading up a shaft to the surface which emerges on the banks of the loading basin. Straight ahead, is a passage which leads deeper into the system, but this part has not yet been fully cleared and tours do not usually visit this part of the workings. On the right hand side is a very low tunnel that you would have to crawl along. At present it goes nowhere interesting and one look down it would be enough to dissuade anyone from further investigation!

Our route is down the short left hand tunnel which slants downhill slightly, and has a dry stone packed wall on its right hand side. After only a few yards and down a step, we find ourselves standing in the main drainage or tailrace tunnel at a point over three quarters of it's way into the tunnel system.

The Tailrace Tunnel.

Rather than turning left and going out, we go right (upstream). In the main drainage passage, the water is about gents wellington boot height - if nobody causes waves it is possible (just) to keep the feet dry! We proceed down another brick lined tunnel but as this section has not yet had all the debris removed, it is not quite such an easy walk as the service tunnel earlier.

The bricks are left behind and the tunnel is more "cave like" at this point, with walls which are far from smooth.

We pass by the base of another shaft and soon a small entrance in the left hand wall can be entered for a view of the only coal seam in the system (don't forget, we are not in the mine itself, merely in the drainage tunnels designed by Brindley). After only a few yards the roof of the tunnel lowers, and daylight can be seen ahead from the wheel chamber where the water first enters the drainage tunnels. This entrance is currently sealed with a barred metal gate.

*Alan Davies removing mud from the tunnels next to the
wheelchamber.*

We retrace our steps returning to the point where we first entered
the drainage tunnel. This time we go downstream.

This section goes right through the Irwell Valley Fault and is tall
and brick lined using up to 7 courses of brick to give it strength. At
this point, the passage has not been cleared of silt and most of the
debris are piled up to one side of the passage, so you may have to
squeeze sideways at some points. Soon you will go past a partial roof
collapse but it is quite safe to walk under it - quickly.

We are soon back at the other entrance to the Square Shaft in the left hand wall, but we carry straight on and duck down under the lowering roof and go down the main tailrace tunnel.

Dave Lane at the junction of the two main tunnels. The Square shaft is to the left, with the Tailrace tunnel to the right. The view is taken from higher up the tailrace tunnel. The "ghostlike" appearance of the writer is due to the fact that this was a "multiple flash" exposure and I only arrived on the scene after the first flash had gone off! The wonders of modern science!

The same view, prior to the Tailrace tunnel being cleared. At this stage it was not known where the right tunnel went but after

clearing the entrance of the tailrace tunnel, the water levels suddenly reduced and the full tailrace tunnel became passable from the river bank to this point.

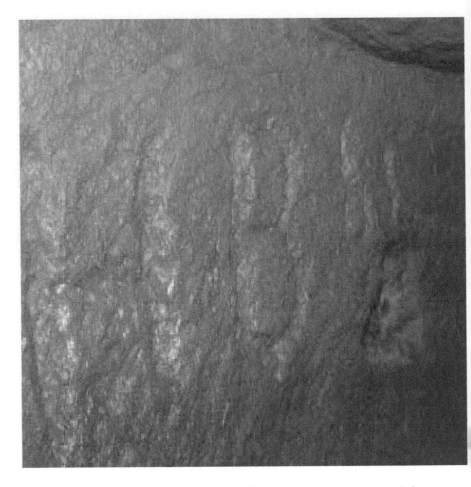

The passage is only low because silt has not yet been cleared from the next 50 yards or so of passage. A miners inscription "HB 65" can be seen carved on the left hand wall. Unfortunately the first two digits are missing from the date, so we don't know whether it reads 1765, 1865 or (most unlikely) 1965

The passage continues at this reduced height for around 100 yards then increases in height quite considerably.

Alan Davies leading a party of youngsters through the "low" section of the tailrace tunnel. Mud not yet cleared is on the left side of the channel.

You can soon stand up straight!

Eric Patella strolling down the tailrace tunnel heading towards the Irwell River exit.

Apart from a couple of very short brick lined sections, this part of the system is once again in solid red sandstone apart from a couple of brick lined sections and is tall, wide and airy - with water on the floor. The miners pick marks can be clearly seen, as can some of the small niches in the walls where they would place their tallow candles. The passage goes under another craftsman built shaft, then heads virtually straight for the open air except for a final bend at which point a further tunnel heads off on the right hand side. The side tunnel is known as "Dave's Tunnel" as is further described in another article. This side tunnel is still filled to the roof with silt.

And that's your trip down the tunnels at Wet Earth!

This description of the Wet Earth tunnels only scratches the surface, for only two of the major tunnels have been described, the Service tunnel and the High tunnel. At many points in the description, other side branches have been mentioned, some blocked, but a number have been fully explored. Those explored tunnels have been photographed and at some future stage full descriptions may be included in another publication.

At the time of writing, you will have to be satisfied with this brief written trip, for the tunnels are currently closed to the public (AND to members of the Wet Earth Exploration Group) for the time being and will probably remain closed for many years.

The underground system was subject to discussions between the Coal Authority (who technically "own" the tunnels), and the City of Salford (who in the past have said they would like to own the tunnels and eventually re-open them to the public – in practice they seem to have washed their hands of the whole matter and nothing has happened for years!). At present everyone involved feels it best to keep out until all legal and safety implications have been sorted out.

Did you know...........

Some of the output from Wet Earth was used in the manufacture of floor tiles at Pilkingtons, the nearby tile and pottery manufacturing firm: Franklyn Shaw writes: *"Large quantities of Pit Marl (called by miners clean dirt) was coming from Newtown and Wet Earth Collieries and stacked on waste ground to be weathered. This was a slate grey colour. This Marl was continually being turned over and raked to a fine tilth to be made ready for grinding and was primarily used for the making of Buff Floor Tiles, and our original Flemish Body and Plastic Cream Body".*

The Visitor Centre under construction. The photographer is unknown.

Wet Earth Colliery. Calendar of events that occurred from the 18th Century.

1710 Michael Heathcote born

1716 James Brindley born

1731 Mathew Fletcher born

1 747/9Mathew Fletcher went to Heathcote at Clifton

1749? Gal Pit sunk

1750 Michael Heathcote married Rachel Edensor. During the wedding festivities the name of Brindley was mentioned which led to the meeting with John Heathcote of Salford.

1751 Brindley commenced work on the tunnel and inverted siphon at Giants Seat, Ringley

1756 Work on the tunnel completed and the pumping scheme at Wet Earth Colliery put into operation

1757 John Edensor Heathcote born

1763 Clifton House constructed by Mathew Fletcher

1772 Death of James Brindley

1790 Mathew Fletcher extended Brindley's feeder channel to connect with the Manchester, Bolton & Bury Canal at Clifton

1805 Downcast shaft sunk and steam winding engine installed

1808 Death of Matthew Fletcher

1822 Death of Sir John Edensor Fletcher

1860 Wet Earth Colliery surveyed by William Nelson

1867 Original wheel replaced by more modern turbine

1910 Wet Earth Drift Mine closed

1923? Ringley weir raised by 2 feet

1924 Turbine wheel dismantled. Water power replaced by steam

1928 Closure of Wet Earth Colliery and Fletchers Canal

1952 Survey carried out to determine line and level of Brindley's tunnel at Ringley Fold

1954 Formation of Bolton and District Joint Sewerage Board and purchase by the Board of the Ringley Fold site and Fletchers Canal

1958 Red Rock Lane diverted, Borrow pit exposed shafts on line of tunnel

1959 Further survey of tunnel

1960 Tunnel sealed off and partially demolished

1963 Siphon head sealed off by brick wall
1964 Ringley Fold Sewerage Treatment works put into operation
1965 Heathcote's house demolished on at Doe Brow
1966 Tunnel and inverted siphon surveyed for record purposes

The Jonas Lindlay Suspension Bridge

Although there is now a fine modern pedestrian suspension bridge (built in 1992) over the Irwell at Giants Seat just upstream of the water treatment outflow, there was a much earlier bridge crossing the river at this point in earlier days.

The earlier bridge was designed and built by Jonas Lindley, a 19th century civil engineer, who was apparently acknowledged at that time to be one of the finest suspension bridge builders in the country. Jonas was born in Ringley and following his apprenticeship at Andrew Knowles's Clifton Hall Colliery he joined the Clifton and Kearsley Coal Company and became the firms foreman carpenter and building consultant.

The Lindlay Bridge spanned the Irwell running from Ringley Brow to Fletchers Canal and the colliery feeder at Giants Seat. Due to the width of the river at this point, it had always been thought that only a stone or brick one, built with two strong piers would suffice but this would have proved too costly. However Jonas decided that he could build a timber structure using massive beams and using lock-coil ropes of great breaking strain. The ropes were passed over cross beams on uprights like giant goal posts and the resultant suspension bridge was completed and was quite capable of of taking any average load. The bridge was only open at certain times and had a gate on the Ringley side allowing the Ringley and Kearsley miners to cross the river on their way to Wet Earth.

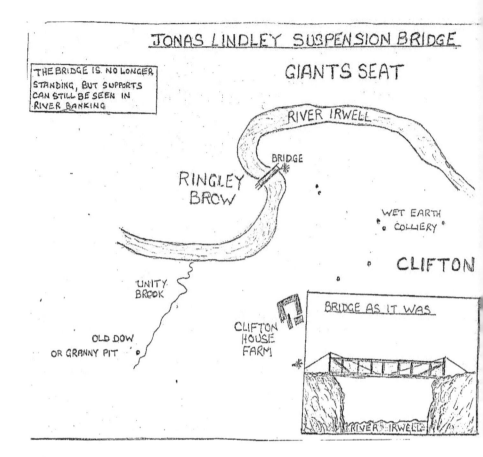

JONAS LINDLEY SUSPENSION BRIDGE

GIANTS SEAT

THE BRIDGE IS NO LONGER STANDING, BUT SUPPORTS CAN STILL BE SEEN IN RIVER BANKING

RIVER IRWELL

BRIDGE

RINGLEY BROW

WET EARTH COLLIERY

CLIFTON

UNITY BROOK

OLD DOW OR GRANNY PIT

CLIFTON HOUSE FARM

BRIDGE AS IT WAS

RIVER IRWELL

Although the bridge is no longer standing, stone supports can still be seen on the Irwell banking. Exact dating of the bridge is not known but it is shown as being in existence on the Ordinace Survey maps of the 1870's. A Mr Edwin Greenhalgh of Kearsley, remembers well seeing the the bridge around 1930 (that is some 2 years after Wet Earth pit closed), when it was finally removed for safety purposes.

The bridge was owned by the Clifton and Kearsly Coal Company. It's main purpose was for the conveyance of timber, animal feeds and agricultural products.

Poor quality copy of an aerial photograph taken of Wet Earth area by the Germans either just before WW2 or during the war. Clifton House Road is visible at the bottom right hand side.

Wet Earth Drift Mine.

The drift mine at Wet Earth (also known as the Day Eye) seems to have been operated as a separate mine from the deep mine, often appearing in reference books as a separate entity. The exact location of the drift entrance has not yet been discovered although with a bit of surveying (from the remains of the rails "near" to the entrance and the air shaft further away in the woods) plus the removal of an awful lot of earth (!) it should not prove too difficult to locate. However, if the entrance were to be found, all indications are that the tunnel would contain very high gas levels making any sort of entry impossible.

The drift mine at Wet Earth opened around the 1880's and closed in 1910. Some 100 yards south of the drift entrance a ventilation shaft had been dug around 90 feet deep but this is now capped. Just over 10 years ago, the depth of the shaft was tested (via some broken brickwork) and a depth of only 75 feet was measured. Testing with a Garforth lamp indicated a severe lack of oxygen even at entry level, so any further investigation of this shaft was halted. There have been no further attempts to effect entry to the drift! Unfortunately no photographs seem to exist of the drift mine and very little written information seems to exist about it.

The drift mine followed the Black seam of coal down from the surface where it outcropped. Tubs were wound up the drift by a large steam winding engine, then travelled over the canal arm on a bridge towards the washery and screens. It is understood that as well as workmen travelling down the drift a sizeable population of rats also found their way down, living off scraps of food left by the men.

One interesting reference to the drift was recorded by Ian Howarth of Swinton who wrote about a lady called Miss Collier who remembers *"visiting the drift mine with her grandfather from being a child until just before the mine closed. She remembers her grandfather going down the drift mine to check the water levels whenever there was a problem with flooding.*
The drift entrance was of brick and the railtracks that led down the mine were set to one side to allow the pit ponies to walk in and out of the mine. The ponies and horses were looked after by Miss

Collier's uncle Tom who lived in a brick house with brick built stables between the mine and Dickie Pea Bridge.

Uncle Tom's job was to look after the pit ponies and horses and to work the ponies on a rota down the mine so that they had approximately one week on and one week off. When the ponies came up the drift at the end of the week they would frisk and jump about in the field just like little children. The ponies were very well groomed.

On May day, all of the ponies and horses were dressed up by the pit men who would stay up all night to groom and decorate them along with all the coal carts washed ready for a procession through Clifton which was then little more than a village. This procession would join in with other carts from local mills and traders".

In the Eccles and Patricroft Journal of 22nd May 1896 it states that:

"100 men and boys at the Day Eye Pit .... Struck work, owing to the firm stopping an allowance of 5s for yardage ...The White Mine is only about 2ft 10 inches thick and the men are struggling to make working the coal pay .... A similar mine is being worked at Manor Pit, Kearsle the men are getting higher wages ...... the employers pay jiggers there to remove the coal .... The Day Eye men would be willing to accept this system"

Alan Davies, the late curator of the Lancashire Mining Museum in Salford gives the following explanatory Notes on the above (reproduced from "Wet Earth Colliery News" – an occasional newsletter of the Wet Earth Exploration Group)

"This may read a bit confusing to some of you, basically yardage was a payment in respect of face advance or tunnel advance over and above a set amount per week. The men in the Day Eye working the thinning seam were producing less coal, the advance wasn't too good and the company was punishing the men for a problem which was not within their control. i.e. geology

The answer was for the union (the Lancashire Miners Federation) to renegotiate yardage for the conditions with Clifton and Kersley Coal Company.

In certain areas of the Lancashire coalfield the constant renegotiating of price lists and yardage must have really kept the union and management busy. Also the union would find itself calling on different coal companies with differing relations with their workforces. No cushy union jobs a century ago"

Another snippet from the past.

In the 1896 mines survey the Wet Earth Drift mine was managed by a William Nelson Jnr and at that time 166 men were working underground with a further 32 on the surface. This compares with the main Wet Earth Mine where 304 were employed underground with 102 on the surface. Wet Earth must have been quite a busy place at the turn of the century.

By 1911 the workforce at Wet Earth had risen to 450 underground with 156 on the surface whilst the Drift was employing only 86 underground and 19 on the surface.

A party walking in the tailrace tunnel.

The River Irwell.

The River Irwell until the early years of the 19th century could boast Salmon, Dace, Chub and even Trout. After around 1825 water quality deteriorated and today very few species survive today.

The greatest recorded flood occurred in 1866 when the maximum flow was estimated at 42,000 tons per minute which is about 113 times the normal flow.

Wet Earth Exploration Group (or at least some of them) – Mid 1990

The main Service Tunnel looking towards the entrance.

Is the Wheel Chamber Brindleys original one?

Although everyone speaks of the present wheel chamber as if it were definitely the one designed and built by Brindley, information has come to light during the past few years which may throw some doubt on this.

At present we have always assumed that Brindleys original plan was to take water from the Irwell at a point opposite to the old Kearsley power station. The water then travelled through underground tunnels on the Northern bank of the river, and then passed over to the Southern bank via a siphon (a sort of underground U-bend!). At the point on the southern bank where the "upcast" siphon shaft is located, Brindley was assumed to have then fed this water into a surface feeder stream which transferred the water high on the river bank and thence to the Wheel Chamber located just to the side of the old Gal Pit, this pit being assumed to be the "original" main shaft of Wet Earth Colliery. Until recently this was the accepted scenario.

However, a few years ago an old map of the area was discovered. The map was not dated. The map clearly shows the siphon upcast plus the feeder stream taking the water to the vicinity of the Gal Pit at Wet Earth (at that period "Wet Earth" was known as "Wet Yard Pit"). However, the map also shows that apart from the siphon supplying water to the feeder stream, it also fed water via an underground tunnel a fairly short distance to the "Old Doe Water Wheel" shaft. This shaft was located on the bend at Giants Seat and is now filled in (with the public footpath directly on top of it!). Presumably, this was a shaft with a water wheel at it's bottom. The waste water from the wheel, was then conveyed back to the river via another underground tunnel passing directly under the Marina and thence to the Irwell.

On the next page is shown a scaled down view of the newly discovered map. The quality of the original map was equally faint! The river and feeder stream can be seen at the top of the map. A dotted line then goes from the siphon upcast to the Old Doe Water Wheel shaft. A further dotted line then goes from that shaft to the Wet Yard Ladder Pit and is clearly marked "Sliding Rods to work pumps"

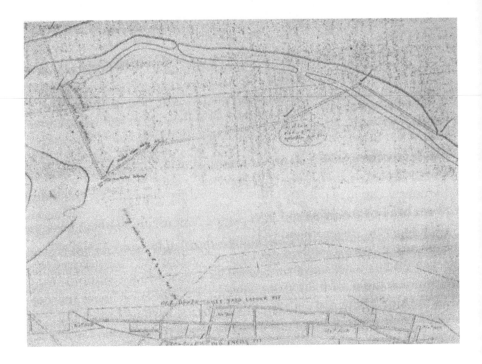

There is no doubt that these tunnels existed. The tunnel from the siphon to the Doe water wheel shaft starts about ten feet down the siphon upcast shaft and was explored some years ago. The difficulties of getting down into the tunnel, plus the glutinous "hard to dig" fill in the tunnels meant that only a very short distance of passageway has been explored and if ever we wanted to carry on digging it would be some distance before the water wheel shaft was reached.

The original water wheel just may still be there!

Part of the outflow tunnel from the water wheel shaft to the river has also been explored but it is now blocked. The permanent blockage was due to the fact that soon after the Marina had been dug (to provide gravel for the building of the nearby motorway), its bed collapsed into the underground tunnel, water rushed into the tunnel under considerable pressure, scoured the tunnel - and emptied the Marina! The hole was plugged with rubbish and concrete and the Marine was refilled. The tunnel has been explored only as far as the plug.

The Water Wheel shaft, served with water by the underground tunnel from the siphon seems, to have operated only as a place to house the water wheel and no coal workings are shown on the map (even though workings are shown on the map in other areas). What **IS** shown on the map however, is that the water wheel operated a series of "sliding rods" over 200 meters in length located on the surface running from the Water Wheel Shaft to a shaft marked as "Old Engine Pit", this being located 150 meters to the North of the present Visitor Centre. This type of moving or sliding rods, operated by a water wheel, has been used in various mining areas of the UK, but nowadays it is very hard to envisage what it must have looked like here at Wet Earth. These rods would have been clearly visible on the surface and must have been quite a size and length – perhaps fairly noisy. There are no signs whatsoever of either the rods or the piers on which they must have been mounted to be seen today. There is however a strange long mound of earth lying on the direct line of where the rods once were in the fenced off farmers field

The big question is ....did the wheel at the bottom of the Doe Water Wheel Shaft precede the wheel in what we now call the Wheel Chamber? Could the Water Wheel Shaft be the original Brindleys water wheel? On the newly found map, although the pumping rods were used adjacent to the Old Engine Pit, there is yet another shaft marked only a few yards it. This was known as the "Wet Yard Ladder Pit". Could this be the "original" Wet Earth colliery which needed urgent draining?

Now that all exploration is currently banned at the site, perhaps we may never learn the truth. If permission were ever granted for exploration to restart, one of the outstanding tasks must be to try to clear the tunnel from the siphon to the Doe Water Wheel Shaft. Who knows what may be found!

Snippet from "an old Clifton Diary" ......

"River up to a great height. Floods on July 13th 1828. The water backed up and reached the Doe Water Wheel Shaft within about 4 inches. August 18th 1828 it was 2 feet higher"

Where does "Dave's Tunnel" go?

The tunnel known as "Daves Tunnel" - (so called because it was being dug by Dave Lane and Dave Holden, both members of the Wet Earth Exploration Group) is a complete and unknown entity. We know neither its purpose nor where it goes!

At the river entrance to the tailrace tunnel, it had long been noted that some ten yards inside the entrance, a further tunnel had been dug in the sandstone which headed off parallel to the River Irwell. This passage was blocked to the roof with silt. The tunnel is about six foot in height and perhaps five foot in width with a box like appearance. It was obviously dug to carry a reasonable amount of water.

Dave Holden (Mr "T") digging in the tunnel. His smile is forced as there could be another mile yet to dig!

There are two theories as to its possible purpose. At the entrance to the tailrace tunnel there are clear signs that boards of wood could be put in place into slots cut into the sandstone. We assume that the wood was used at times when the river water level was rising in order to stop the river water entering the main tunnel. We further assumed that Dave's Tunnel was a means by which the water coming down the tailrace tunnel from the Wheel Chamber, could be redirected

lower down the Irwell valley and discharged back into the river at a
point higher than the now swollen River Irwell water surface. That
is one theory.

There is yet another theory. There have always been rumours that
the nearby pit at Botany Bay also had an underground water wheel
used for pumping purposes. Could it be that Dave's Tunnel goes all
the way to Botany Bay to provide extra water for the operation of
this wheel. This is not as far fetched as it may sound, for although
only a short distance of the tunnel has been dug out, we DO know
that it continues for a great distance. Maps indicate its presence for
at least a distance of over 400 meters with no signs of a discharge
point into the Irwell. Whilst investigating tunnels lower down the
river, it is apparent that Dave's Tunnel intersects these passages also.
No tunnel has yet been discovered which is an obvious discharge
point into the river for the water travelling down Daves Tunnel from
Wet Earth.

So where does it go? We don't know! It could easily run underground
parallel to the river even past the motorway bridge, in which case the
water just MAY have been used at Botany Bay Pit as a source or
power as has been theorised by some in the past. Alternatively, it may
end at the Wet Earth side of the motorway bridge and merely
discharge into the river. Without further underground work and
exploration we will never learn the truth. Yet another of the mysteries
of Wet Earth just waiting to be discovered

The Siphon and Siphon Chamber.

The siphon under the Irwell was one of the stokes of genius of James
Brindley, the designer of the whole water system at Wet Earth. He
was faced with the problem of how to get water from an underground
tunnel on the northern bank of the Irwell across to the opposite
bank.

Many have asked why Brindley did not merely bring the water from
the Ringley weir on the southern side of the river in the first place. No
exact answer is known, but it is thought that either legal permission
was unobtainable from adjoining landowners, or the rock

strata was unsuitable. The latter answer is thought unlikely, as the digging of a tunnel may in fact, not have been necessary as a deep sided water course could have been constructed. The landowners were more likely to have been the reason for the tunnel detour to the northern bank of the river.

Whatever the reason, the water was taken from the Ringley weir on the northern bank and it immediately entered a tunnel via sluice gates (the current sluice gates are of modern construction). The tunnel passed underneath what is now the site of the water treatment plant until it reached the bank of the Irwell at Giants Seat. The bulk of this passage is now either filled in or is totally inaccessible.

On the river banks two vertical shafts were dug, one on either side of the river, down to a depth of around 55 feet. The bases of the shafts were connected with a horizontal tunnel which passed under the bed of the Irwell. The depth of rock between the bed of the river and the horizontal tunnel is not known but measurements taken in the 1960's indicate that it is perhaps 10 to 15 feet.

The day the cave diver came to check the condition of the siphon under the Irwell.

On the northern bank, the underground feeder from the weir led straight to the siphon head where the water plunged down the vertical shaft, passed underneath the river and back up the shaft on the opposite bank. On the northern bank a "washout" tunnel runs from the siphon head to the bank of the Irwell. It is believed that the washout tunnel was equipped with sluice gates, operated from the surface, which could be used to allow the water to exit to the river bank instead of passing to the syphon shaft. The top of the syphon shaft is now sealed with brickwork (well, sort of!) Several years ago a cave diver braved the siphon waters to see whether there was still a "through route" under the river. The siphon was found to be totally blocked with silt and debris.

On the Wet Earth bank of the river, although the vertical shaft goes to the surface (where it is very securely capped), the water entered an impressive brick lined chamber before it passed into daylight to form the feeder canal high on the river bank. The brick lined chamber is in perfect condition and although a little dangerous, it is still possible to walk through the chamber and to peer down the vertical siphon shaft which still contains water.

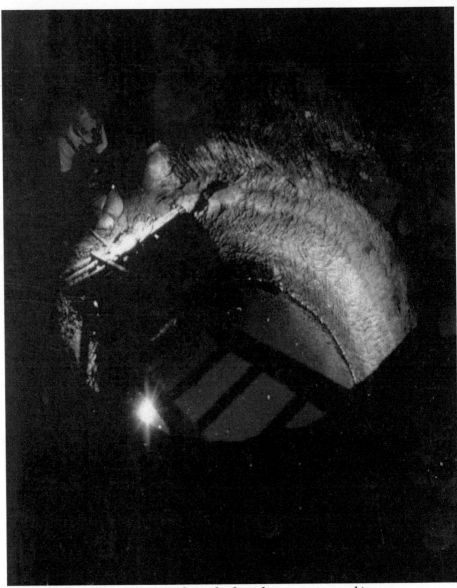

*Looking down the upcast siphon shaft with someone working
at the side tunnel entrance mentioned below.*

Whilst looking down the shaft, one notices a small tunnel in the
southern wall, this being the one which we believe leads to the Doe
Water Wheel Shaft mentioned in an earlier chapter. The tunnel has
been excavated for only a short distance and working conditions in
this tunnel were pretty awful. The siphon chamber is securely locked
behind a steel door and is currently not available for public viewing.

WISHING STONE

This stone, which was probably used as
a marking stone and which is contemporary with the Clifton incense cup in the
British Museum, lies opposite the arch
at the bottom of Clifton House Road.

There is evidence that it has been in
its present position for the past 200
years. It has always been referred to
as the "Wishing Stone".

Photo of the "Wishing Stone" in its original location. The Wet Earth Exploration Group moved the Stone from its partially hidden resting place to a point next to the Visitor Centre. This was a wrong decision! The stone was broken by vandals within 6 months.

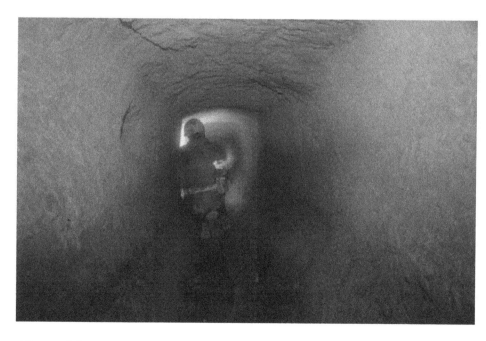

View of the main "Service Tunnel" prior to silt being removed.
The tunnel is now twice the height shown in the photo.

Gas danger shuts 'child tour' mine

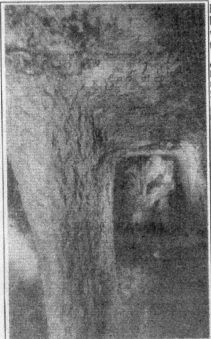

UPSET by closure decision . . . Alan Davies underground at Clifton

HUNDREDS of children's lives may have been at risk from lethal gas when they went down a 250-year-old mineshaft on trips run by a voluntary group.

Wet Earth Colliery Explorations has now been told to shut down the 1,000-metre water drainage shaft at Clifton Country Park, which has been seen by scores of school groups, Guides and Scouts since it was opened for organised visits seven years ago.

Mining experts said "mine gas, mine water, unstable shaft-fill and control of access" could pose potential dangers.

A spokesman for International Mining Consultants Ltd said a recent survey of the underground workings led to their decision.

"After consultation with the Coal Authority," he said, "we wish to make clear that access into the workings should cease."

The drainage shafts in the country park near Swinton were first built as part of James Brindley's water wheel complex in 1750.

Brindley was the mastermind behind the Bridgewater Canal and the area was being considered as a potential tourist attraction.

Now health and safety chiefs at Salford city council are to launch an investigation. A spokesman said: "We are very concerned at the findings and we will close the colliery while we review and investigate the matter."

But Lancashire Mining Museum curator Alan Davies has rejected demands that the old shafts should be closed.

"We worked long and hard to draw up a rigorous code of prac-

By Jaya Narain

tice with health and safety officers," he said, "and we would never have allowed people down if there had been any danger.

"We dispute using the word 'workings,' as this isn't the case."

Mr Davies set up the 20-strong Wet Earth Colliery Exploration Group — trained engineers with years of experience who work voluntarily to run the site.

"The last thing we would have done is take brownie groups down the shaft if we weren't convinced it was safe," he said. "We've had expert training on what to do in emergencies and are confident the shaft poses no danger."

A spokesman for the Coal Authority said no unsafe areas had been directly pinpointed, although a further survey might highlight dangerous spots.

He said a survey would map shafts and galleries to examine the possibility of mine gas and water causing a potential hazard.

The Manchester Evening News article from 1997 which effectively closed down the tunnels. Virtually every single statement made by the reporter was either totally wrong, inaccurate or was an extreme case of "creative" reporting!

The only two known existing photographs of Wet Earth Colliery.

Wet Earth Colliery Photograph: A description by Mr J Robinson

The pit head as we see it in the photograph has been turned round 180 degrees. This was done in one weekend c. 1904, by the colliery carpenter. It was placed against a new engine house (on left) which contained a larger engine so that the deeper seams could be reached. The shaft contains a 4 deck cage, each deck carrying one tub of approximately 7 cwt capacity. Steps at the left of the headgear give access to the upper cage decks, usually reserved for boys. The original engine house for the shaft (on right) now became the slant winding house (pronounced "slaunt). This was a haulage engine whose endless rope ran down the shaft in a box connected to a endless rope haulage and ran back up again. It was this that was involved with the fatal accident of Mr Jones *(full description of the accident in the Swinton Journal Feb 3rd 1911).* The rope went down the shaft via a small pulley located in between in between the two main winding pulleys.

The engine in front of the slant winding house was a kibble engine (possibly a sinking engine G.P.). This operated a kibble in the shaft for repairs etc. It was this engine which lowered Mr Jones, but because of the poor maintenance in it, the gears were worn and they slipped out of mesh plunging the kibble down the shaft onto the blocked cage. Braking was by a large band around the side of the drum.

The windlass situated next to this was used for lowering large pieces of machinery down the shaft that would not fit into the cage e.g. a Hopkinson compressed air disc coal cutter. Similar hand windlasses were used underground for winding a set of tubs up an incline.

Between the kibble engine drum and the foot of the headgear can be seen two chains. This is the endless chain haulage system that took coal and dirt to the "hand picks" i.e. where dirt would be broken off the saleable coal. The waste was called "burgey". The colliery would raise up to 3,000 tubs a day. The waste would be tipped over shallow land beyond the pit. It was a stipulation that this had to be levelled and covered with topsoil as soon as possible. This was done and vegetables were often grown there.

The chimney of the Old Furnace Pit can be seen beyond the new engine house. Ventilation used to be caused by an underground furnace at the bottom of this shaft but a fan engine was later installed (thought to be an old mill engine with rope drives to the fan. The Old Furnace Shaft then became an extra escape route and was actually used as such during Mr Jones' accident. Three men had to inspect this shaft (in a kibble) every Friday. On the far side is the steam pipe to the winding engine.

There are thought to have been 47 seams of coal on this site (not all workable). The colliery closed through lack of sales with the collapse of export markets. Production was still high at closure, indeed Cannel Mine had recently been developed. An underground water pump was installed around 1916 (Mr Robinson started in 1914). Some profitable seams closed down in the war (19 14-18) due to state control and more difficult seams were worked (i.e a fiddle"!) In the same vein about 12 coal trucks with the inferior coal from Astley Green were brought to Wet Earth each day and mixed with the Wet Earth coal to dilute the quality.

Also during the war, all the horses were confiscated and mules were given back in their place. They were used to draw coal barges along Fletchers Canal but were very stubborn. Instead of easing onto the load they tried to pull off violently. This often ended in them being drawn into the canal. As it had quite a high towpath, many were drowned.

The colliery had 10 boilers, two of which were closed down at any one time. 4 were low pressure boilers (up to 50 psi). These were used for the fan engine and winders.

The man with the moustache looking at the camera might be Alf Ashton

Mr James Robinson
Clifton
Details noted down by G Preece 3.11.1982

Fletchers Folly.

Fletchers Folly is the name given to the chimney which is perched on the hillside above Wet Earth Colliery with no apparent link to anything.
Ellis Fletcher (1765-1834) took over the operation of the colliery after his uncle Mathew Fletcher (173 1-1808) died. He is thought to have introduced stream winding at the pit in 1805 when the downcast shaft was dug.

Rather than construct a very tall chimney near to the boilers to clear the level of housing on the top road he had the idea of mounting a chimney of smaller dimensions nearer to the road. By having a flue connection (of about 4 feet high by 2 feet wide) back to the boilers a good draught could be obtained, similar to one achieved with a tall chimney.

The chimney was built round about 1805 and raised in the mid 19th century. By the 1890's a replacement chimney was built at the later boiler house, of standard height. Fletcher's chimney was then lowered for safety reasons back to its original height of today.

The chimney is one of the earliest industrial examples to have survived in the North West and was restored in 1988/9. The use of ornamentation could have been through the landowner Heathcote's Staffordshire pottery connection.

Bit's & Pieces from the Irwell Valley at Clifton.

Whilst pottering around in the valley near Clifton Country Park, the group often comes across all sorts of bits and pieces which may be of interest to others, but which are not strictly to do with the colliery. This page will be reserved for those bits and pieces! Although this article is headed "Wet Earth Colliery Exploration Group", that group is in fact no longer in existence. The article is compiled purely by a group of individuals (many of whom were never even members of the original Exploration Group) who care about the Wet Earth Site and its environs.

Wet Earth Pit Tally (pit tally's are sometimes known as "pit checks")

The photograph shows a "pit tally" (sometimes known as a "pit check") issued to underground workers at Wet Earth. The initials stand for the owners of the Colliery, the Clifton and Kearsley Coal Company Ltd. This particular style of tally may also have been available at other pits owned by the C & K company and may not be unique to Wet Earth. These were made in brass and in most collieries, one was issued to each miner, and his individual number was stamped on the front. When the miner went underground, the tally would be left at the surface. In this way it was always possible for management to see exactly how many people were underground at any time and to know who they were.

The tally system worked slightly differently at different collieries (sometimes the tally was left in return for a lamp, sometimes it was handed in before the miner entered the cage to go underground etc).

Whilst exploring the tunnels at Wet Earth, three tally's were found. These are now in safe keeping. So far as I am aware these are the only known examples of this particular pit tally (although I will check with other tally collectors to see if anyone else knows of further copies).

Found 12.5.2001 (somewhere near the visitor centre!)

The valley was once a thriving community with cottages, a large coal mine, railway sidings, mine owners house etc. In those days, there was no municipal refuse removal service, so unwanted household or industrial rubbish were just tipped wherever it may have seemed appropriate at that time.

When searching through old rubbish sites in the valley, members of the Exploration Society have come across a number of 19th century bottles, bowls and stems from clay pipes, along with large amounts of broken pottery of all descriptions.

One interesting find amongst the "household rubbish" is a fair old quantity of old oyster or similar shells!!! Either we have discovered the remains of the lord of the households junk, or we have found out that the Irwell once contained freshwater shellfish which were freely eaten by the locals. Anyone else any other ideas?

The Clifton dump!

People have been e-mailing me about the "dig" mentioned above, asking the age of what was found, why was it dumped where it was, what type of things were found etc.

Well, now you can see the "dig"! After the country park authorities
requested that digging stop, the site has not been revisited -
although at that time the site was exhausted. The items found were
about 4 to 6 feet below the present surface, located very near to
an ancient pathway.

Examination of the artefacts produced large amounts of broken
pottery, the ink or cream jars shown above, are the only form of
pottery found intact. Although bottles were found, there were
none which ever contained alcohol. Oyster type shells were found
in abundance but by far the most surprising finds were the vast
amount of clay pipes discovered. When digging other dumps or tips
in the area, one often finds clay pipe, but nowhere has anyone found
so many in such a tiny area. We can think of no easy explanation as
to why they exist in such numbers in such a place - very few pipe
stems or parts of stems were found. A total of 86 clay bowls were
unearthed - the longest stem found was around 6 inches. Some of
the last pieces of pottery discovered at the site are possibly the best
for dating the dump- Salt glazed stoneware from Bourne & Sons
Denby & Codnor Park Pottery which can definately be dated to the
1833 to 1861 period. One of the clay pipes has a makers cartouch

which will give a 10 year date period once we can finally get it identified. I'll put more news on about the finds when more information is forthcoming. **7.9.01 Latest news on the clay bowl mentioned above. The clay pipe collectors society feel that this pipe with the cartouch is actually Dutch and not English. Their reference document "De Nederlandse Kleipijp" by D H Duco identifies the bowl and mark to range between 1680 and 1750. They cannot be more precise because even they don't have the exact markings on another pipe. Now that's a turn-up for the books!!!!!**

Although all of the finds are in individuals homes, they will all be made available should the Park Authorities ever wish to mount an exhibition of archaeological items found in the valley. All involved in the finds, feel that the public should be kept fully aware at what has been discovered, and this web site is intended to diseminate this information to anyone interested in the Valley. No excavations or explorations of any type are currently being conducted in the valley so far as I am aware.

The site of the "old" ford

Did you know that on the banks of the Irwell at Wet Earth you can still find the remains of the ancient "paved" trackway on the Clifton side of the river, leading right down to the ford which once existed at that site. If only the moss and weeds currently covering the "track" were to be cleared away by someone, then there'd be yet another bit of local history restored. This would then be one bit of **real** history in the country park that the authorities could actually leave on display to the public. Most of the rest are either closed down, padlocked off or you're forbidden to get into them.

Grab your chance folks, look at the old fording point before "they" decide the site is 1. Too dangerous for the public 2. Contravenes the health and safety regulations 3. Is owned by Salford and is therefore henceforth up for sale etc! Go and see it whilst the last bit remaining is still there! To be honest this particular bit of track was so well built that it'll probably last a few decades yet - the upstream side is getting slowly swept away by floods so if you want to volunteer a rebuild! There is no sign of a track-way on the opposite bank which is covered in extensive sediment. Long before the present suspension bridge was erected there used to be another bridge on exactly the same site. You can see the original sandstone support brickwork beneath the present bridge. Nice ferns on the Clifton bank especially the tiny ones under the overhanging rock. Don't touch them .... leave them for others to observe.

Bygone names preserved.

At various places on the riverbank between the motorway bridge and Giants Seat, there are a large number of initials carved into the soft red sandstone rock at various points down at river level. The bulk of them seem to appear around the various tunnel entrances. A number of the initials are dated but some of them are obviously of much an older era and have been hacked out with miners picks. Next to one tunnel entrance, the initials "HB" appear, obviously made by a miners pick. This one is interesting for the same initials appear within the main Wet Earth tunnels and bear the same style and pickmarks. Could this "HB" be our areas original graffiti merchant?

See the river in a different light and from a new viewpoint!

Virtually everyone views the Irwell within the Clifton Country Park from the riverside path high up on it's banks. In summer when the water level is low, why not view it all from a different viewpoint and do something slightly different. Take your wellies and walk down the river at the actual edge of the water or even paddling in it. If you drop down the Clifton banking to river level somewhere round about opposite the Nursery on the opposite bank then you'll find a different world. Using the floor of the river and bits of the banking you can "fairly safely" walk right down the river to the M60 from this point apart from a couple of places where you may have to climb up the river bank. This walk is NOT suitable for very young children.

Yeah yeah, ... I know there's an element of danger, I know that you'll probably need a tetanus injection if you fall in the river but go on - be a devil - do something the authorities wouldn't approve of - and have a wonderful day. On a summers day, it's adventurous, fascinating and most of you would love the experience. Try to spot some of the carved initials on the rock. Look for the tiny fish (yup, they really ARE there). Hey, I know it's not gorge scrambling in the Lake District but what do you want here in Salford!

A Brief description of the Wheelchamber.

The wheelchamber can be viewed from outside the railings surrounding it, from where most of the important features can be seen. There is no general access to the chamber via the spiral staircase - other than on an organised tour due to the possible presence of gas at the bottom.

General view of the wheelchamber area. The "original" deep shaft of Gal Pit is on the right. The wheelchamber is surrounded by a steel fence with a spiral staircase inside it. The wheelchamber is kept securely locked and visits are only allowed with an official organised group.

The wheelchamber is situated next to the original Gal Pit which lies alongside. The Gal Pit still exists but is securely capped and there is no longer any access to it either from the top of from the drainage tunnels nearby. The view down the wheelchamber is fairly restricted due to the large horizontal girders that span it near to surface level. However, if you walk slowly round the chamber on the surface and peer down you should be able to see most of the things described below.

Standing on the East Side of the chamber (the side where the entrance to spiral staircase is) and look at the left hand wall you should see the large brick arch behind the cast iron tank arrangement. This is known as the penstock tunnel and supplied water to the wheel chamber from the canal loading basin. The portion of tunnel from this penstock arch back to the loading basin, is blocked due to a large collapse halfway down the passage.

Notice the iron channels alongside the brick arch. These once held oak boards making up a large door which could stop off the water supply to the wheel chamber if maintenance work needed to be carried out. Near the top of the wall, one of the two pulley wheels has survived, these being used to raise and lower the oak door.

The tank arrangement would not have been in place when the original waterwheel was in operation. Its purpose was to supply a water turbine that replaced the wheel soon after 1867 (visible from the other side). The large cast iron pipes at either side of the tank are thought to have supplied water to other turbines within the chamber.

View into the wheelchamber showing the penstock entrance and the iron header tank.

To the lower right of the tank you can see a small square hole in the wall. This meets up with a tunnel from the base of the tank and drained off water before it could enter the turbine. This tunnel also meets the tailrace tunnel from the wheel chamber, the two square exits for which can be seen at the bottom centre of the chamber. These two exits for the water have now been sealed with metal grills.

Intersecting the top of one of these exits you should be able to make out the scour mark in the wall of the original waterwheel. This carries on until meeting the large cross-girder spanning the semi-circular aperture in the eastern wall of the chamber. The scour mark indicates a wheel of approximately 22 feet in diameter. The mark may have been caused by the wheel drifting on its bearings, perhaps due to subsidence.

The fact that the scour mark is intersected by the large cross-girder tells us that possibly both the adjacent chamber and girder work date to after 1867 when the turbines were installed. The huge gritstone blocks in the wall are thought to be part of the original structure of 1749.50, the stone not being of local origin.

Looking to the southern wall of the chamber on your right you can see modern girders holding back the original retaining wall which was found to be in poor condition. Just behind the third girder from the bottom you should be able to see a small metal plate tucked in the corner. Behind the plate is a brick lined culvert about 8 feet long, found behind patched up brickwork. This linked up with the 18th century Gal Pit shaft of 100 yards in depth, the top of which can be seen as a circle of brickwork on the surface.

Water raised up the Gal Pit shaft, made its way along this culvert and emptied into the wheel chamber, joining water used to drive the wheel, draining back to the River Irwell via the tailrace tunnels.

Moving over to the opposite side of the waterwheel chamber you can see at the bottom right the turbine excavated by the Wet Earth Exploration Group. Notice how it is keyed into the brick pillars. Water entered the volute casing of the turbine at this point and spiralled round clockwise until reaching the central section where it hit guide vanes. These directed the water onto the turbine blades, producing rotary motion of the central drive shaft. The guide vanes could be adjusted to vary the speed of the turbine and its power output.

Power produced could then be used to drive pumps via bevel gearing or other equipment via belt drives and pully shafting. The girder work within the chamber was associated with this equipment.

The turbine was probably produced by Gilkes of Kendal after 1867. The firm still makes turbines today, exporting worldwide. Gilkes made other turbines used on the Wet Earth site, for example the one on the riverbank.

Penstock entrance in the loading basin. Photo taken during restoration work in the early 1990's.

The Riverside Turbine.

At a point on the feeder stream, partway between the siphon upcast shaft and the canal arm leading to the loading basin, a certain amount of water was diverted along a channel to a drop tube linked to a turbine on the riverbank. The machinery was housed within a large shed built on the river bank. The turbine must have been installed around the 1880's and was probably made by Gilkes of Kendal. It is known for certain that they supplied a similar turbine close to Pilkingtons Tile Works and probably also supplied the turbine of the 1860's which replaced the waterwheel at the colliery.

Water entered via the 31 inch tube you can still see the remains of, then dropped 23 feet to the vortex type turbine. Water entered the turbine casing at the outer edge and was then guided towards the turbine blades, thus turning the drive shaft, producing about 8 to 10 horse power.

Power from this particular turbine was used to drive a ram pump, the remains of which were found during excavations. This pumped water back up again under pressure. The water could then be used at the coal washery, or for supplying boiler feed lodges.

Looking downstream, the turbine house is just visible in the centre.

Although the Wet Earth Colliery Exploration Group excavated the turbine some years ago, the river has once again covered it over with silt. You should still be able to find it vaguely visible on the riverbank.

Fletchers Canal.

Fletchers Canal, so called after Mathew Fletcher (1731-1808), the driving force behind the funding, engineering and establishment of the Manchester Bolton and Bury Canal. Fletchers canal was in use by 1794. Matthew worked coal under lease from the Clifton landowner Sir John Edsinor Heathcote (b 1695) as well as owning a great deal of land in the area.

To the east, Botany Bay Colliery, also owned by Mathew Fletcher, was situated (where the canal had a side branch underground similar to Worsley Delph). Beyond Botany Bay Clifton Aqueduct linked Fletchers Canal with the Manchester Bolton and Bury Canal, just past present day Pilkington Tile Works. Cal eventually reached the Oldfield Road terminus at Salford supplying industries such as cotton spinning, iron founding and brewing.

At Wet Earth Colliery, Mathew Fletcher had by 1791 a boat building and repair yard, complete with saw pit, joiners shop and blacksmiths shop.

Back in the 18th century coal barges working on this system cost around £40-75, with a length of approx 68 feet by 7 feet wide and having a maximum draught of 3 f33t 6 inches. By the turn of the 20th century the type of those sunk in the canal near to Wet Earth could contain ten wooden boxes each holding up to 1.5 tons of coal, a total load of 15 tons. Some of the sunken barges still contain boxes and suspension chains.

Serious subsidence damage occurred in 1880 due to mining operations with the canal closing for 7 months. In 1905 142,905 tons of coal passed along Fletchers Canal.

Wet Earth colliery closed in 1928. Water still passed through Brindleys siphon and passed over the aqueduct until breaches in the Bolton Bury canal near Little Lever were left unrepaired in 1936. After the war the section of canal from the aqueduct to Fletchers Canal was filled with clay waste. A breach from the 1950's (still visible today) within Fletchers Canal also meant the loss of the bulk of water in the system.

The demolition of Brindleys tunnel in 1960 from Ringley weir meant the eventual loss of water in both feeder stream and canal. Over forty barges from the Clifton fleet lie sunken today in the canal, from a total compliment of nearly 200.

Colliery Loading Basin and dry dock.

A side arm of Fletchers Canal turned towards Wet Earth Colliery at the junction of that canal and the siphon feeder stream. The land at this point formed part of the entry into the colliery arm and was filled in when material was removed from the present lake area for the construction in 1970.

A recently discovered plan of this area dated 1837 shows Mathew Fletcher's enlargement of the feeder stream to the waterwheel into a canal loading basin of circa 1790 still had a natural contour compared with the engineered layout of the mid 19th century visible today.

The end of the loading basin was quite complex, with two sluices and an overflow draining into tunnels below that were linked with the river. Here also was the drydock and boat repair yard of circa 1790, the railway bridge of circa 1900 and a travelling crane used to unload colliery materials such as pit props brought in by either boat or rail. A simple jib crane was also at this point, used to place timbers into the pinch point should the loading basin need to be drained totally.

Around and underneath the loading basin are many underground tunnels that are associated, in the main, with the removal of water from the waterwheel, the overflow from the loading basin and also the water from the dry dock.

Fred Dibnah filming at Wet Earth for the "Industrial Age" series shown on BBC2.

Wheatsheaf Colliery (Pendlebury Colliery).

Wheatsheaf's official name was Pendlebury Colliery but in most records it has always been referred to as Wheatsheaf Colliery taking its name from the nearby Wheatsheaf public house.

The two shafts were dug in 1846 by Andrew Knowles and these continued in use throughout the whole history of the mine. The two 10 foot diameter shafts lay 24 yards apart and were both sunk to a depth of 413 yards to intercept the Rams Mine coal seam. Whilst digging the shafts, incoming water became a major problem and the middle 140 yard section of the shafts had to be lined with cast iron tubing to restrict the flow. Although the top and base of the shafts are brick lined, incoming water had to be collected and deposited at the bottom of the two shafts.

Some forty years after the mine first opened, the Number 1 shaft was deepened to the Doe Mine seam at a depth of 602 yards although the Number 2 shaft always remained at its original depth.

The photo was taken around 1863 prior to the alterations mentioned below.

The winding engine, made by J Musgrave of Bolton was first installed in 1847 and this engine remained in use for almost 100 years until it was replaced in 1944. It was a single cylinder engine driving two drums designed for use with flat ropes and the one engine served both shafts with a single cage in each shaft. In 1868 both the engine and Number 2 shaft were modified in order to wind two cages in this shaft and the wooden headgear of Number 2 shaft was also rebuilt at this time. In the same year, the Number 1 shaft was fitted with a separate twin cylinder engine (from the same maker) and could wind 2.25 tons an hour from the base of the 600 yard deepened shaft. The new pitch pine wooden headgear remained in use until 1950.

When the colliery changed hands in 1929 improvements were made throughout the mine, new ventilation, new tunnels, better transport, new pit bottoms etc and the coal winding was concentrated on the Number 1 shaft. The better ventilation in the mine enabled the coal face cutting equipment to be fully electrified. In 1944 a second-hand engine from Highley Colliery in Shropshire was installed for Number 2 shaft in a new engine house and new steel headgear was fitted. Number 1 shaft was modernised in 1950 with another second-hand engine, new steel headgear, new engine house, large capacity skips etc

Originally the mine was drained of water using a number of small steam driven pumps but in 1891 a larger one was installed underground to back up the smaller pumps. The new pump was built by Walker brothers who also provided a new ventilating fan around the same time. Prior to the arrival of the fans, the mine was ventilated by using a furnace at the bottom of the Number 2 shaft. In 1875 a new set of furnaces were installed and these remained in position until 1960 at the end of the pits life.

A later view of Wheatsheaf Colliery taken around 1900.

At the bottom of Number 2 shaft were 4 boilers producing steam for the haulage engines, air compressors and water pumps, three were Lancashire boilers and one Cornish boiler these being in use until around 1900.

An oil painting that used to be at the Salford Mining Museum which shows Wheatsheaf around 1875 after the modernisation. The building on the right is the Wheatsheaf public house (and closed in 1937)

Various coal seams were worked during the life of the colliery and when closed it was working the Crombouke and Windmill Mine seams. At that time there were 910 people working on the site.

During the collieries life, the pit was owned initially by various Knowles family partnerships until 1873 when it passed to Andrew Knowles & Sons Ltd. Between 1929 and 1947 it was owned by

Manchester Collieries Ltd until it was nationalised under the National Coal Board and it finally closed in 1961.

Number 2 shaft, Wheatsheaf Colliery 1926

From the earliest times, much of the coal output from Wheatsheaf was sold directly to local people from the pit head yard, but in later years, rail links were installed in the nearby Irwell Valley with the Wheatsheaf coal travelling via a tramway down the hillside to the LNWR railway adjacent to Clifton Hall Colliery where a new washery and screening plant had been built around 1873. Initially this was a single tracked tramway running directly from the pit yard, down the hill via a short tunnel. The loaded trams were gravity powered and the empty tubs were hauled back using a vertical table engine located in the colliery.

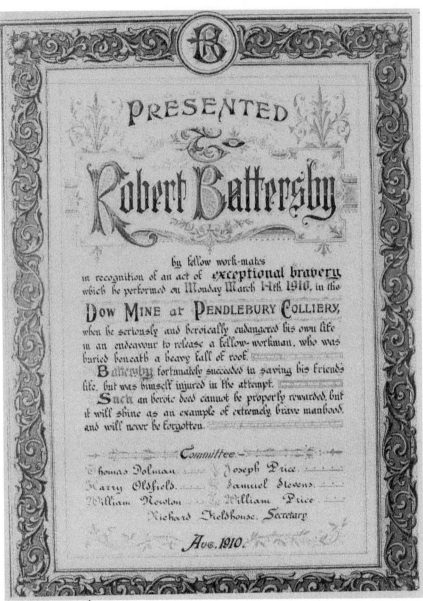

PRESENTED

Robert Battersby

by fellow work-mates in recognition of an act of exceptional bravery which he performed on Monday March 14th. 1910, in the DOW MINE at PENDLEBURY COLLIERY, when he seriously and heroically endangered his own life in an endeavour to release a fellow-workman, who was buried beneath a heavy fall of roof.

Battersby fortunately succeeded in saving his friend's life, but was himself injured in the attempt.

Such an heroic deed cannot be properly rewarded, but it will shine as an example of extremely brave manhood, and will never be forgotten.

— Committee —

Thomas Dolman .... Joseph Price.
Harry Oldfield. .... Samuel Stevens.
William Newton .... William Price.
Richard Fieldhouse, Secretary.

Aug. 1910.

On March 14th 1910 a roof fall occurred in the Dow Mine seam at Wheatsheaf and he was rescued by the recipient of this illuminated address, Mr Robert Battersby. (the late lamented Salford Mining Museum).

Wheatsheaf Colliery intersected a number of different coal seams, Binn, Shuttle, Cranbouke, Rams, White Mine, Black Mine and Doe. It did not work the Five Quarters which lay below the Doe seam. In the main, the rocks in the mine are (apart from the coal) various shales and mudstones but the shafts do pass through a fairly thick band of Peel Hall Rock (sandstone) directly above the Black and White Mines. Shales wound from the pit were used to produce bricks

Although I've never been able to trace any, apparently (according to L H Tonks book "The Geology of the Manchester Coalfield") many fossils were collected from Wheatsheaf at six different levels:

1. Upper tunnel (Bin to Rams), close to the Bin Mine.
2. Lower level tunnel (Rams to Doe), immediately above the Doe, near end of tunnel.
3. A little lower than at 2.
4. Lower level tunnel, 175 foot below Rams Mine, 40 foot below the Lower Yard Mine
5. Lower Level tunnel, 55 ft above the Black or Gingham Mine, 350 ft below Rams Mine, 260 ft above Doe.
6. Lower level tunnel, 405 ft below Rams Mine, 200 ft above Doe Mine. Just below the Black or Gingham Mine.

A photo of the Wheatsheaf main haulage road (taken about 1938). Photo Mr D Owen.

When Manchester Collieries took over Wheatsheaf, apart from the improvements at the colliery itself, the tramway to the valley rail link was also modernised. The tramway tunnel was opened out and the single track was upgraded to a double track from the pit yard to Clifton Hall (by this time Clifton Hall Colliery had closed) and a duel track rail line was laid to the Wheatsheaf washeries. The Wheatsheaf screening plant was also enlarged and modernised.

In 1957, Wheatsheaf was linked by tunnel to Newtown Colliery and the coal from both mines was lifted at Wheatsheaf, passed down the tramway (some coal sales were however still being directly from the mine yard) to the Wheatsheaf screens and then on to the washeries at Outwood. There was a tubway which ran to the old Clifton Hall Colliery and this was retained and used to carry Wheatsheaf waste to the east side of the main railway.

Despite all the attempts to improve the colliery and link it to neighbouring mines, Wheatsheaf was closed down in 1961.

Wheatsheaf Coal Seams & distance from surface.

	Ft	Ins
Coal	708	6
Coal	723	10
Bin Mine	913	4
Shuttle Mine	1020	11
Crumbouke Mine	1026	11
Rams Mine	1194	4
White Mine	1505	9
Black Mine	1577	2
Dow Mine (Doe Mine)	1773	5
Shaft Bottom	1775	3

The rear of Pilkingtons backing onto Fletchers Canal

Pilkington's Tile and Pottery Co. Ltd., Clifton Junction

CLIFTON POTTERIES

88. Pilkington's Tile & Pottery Works, Clifton.

"Holt, Pendlebury"

Surface workers from Wet Earth colliery photographed around 1900.

Aerial view of the Ringley Bridges area.

Manchester Road with Clifton marina in the background.

Rake lane area, Pilkingtons and the M60 motorway.

APPALLING
COLLIERY EXPLOSION
AT KERSLEY

FORTY-THREE LIVES LOST

It is with regret that we have today to record the particulars of the most appalling colliery explosion which has ever occurred in this district. The scene of the disaster, which took place soon after one o'clock on Tuesday afternoon, was at Messrs. J. F. Scott and Co's, Unity Brook Colliery, Kersley, and not less than forty-three lives have been sacrificed. The accidents in January and February of last year at the Stonehill Colliery, Farnworth, and at Fogg's Pit, Darcy Lever, resulted altogether in the loss of 28 lives. Although by the explosion on Tuesday more lives were sacrificed, yet it was unaccompanied by one distressing feature of last year's disasters – the pit did not catch fire, and therefore there was from the first a probability of earlier recovery of the bodies.

The colliery which is a comparatively new one, having only been worked for between nine and ten years, is situated almost adjoining the extensive collieries of the Clifton and Kersley Colliery Company, and about 300 hundred yards from the high road between Bolton and Manchester. During the principal portion of the time that the pit has been working the Trencherbone Mine, which lies at a depth of 340 yards below the surface, has been worked, and it was only about - months since that the shaft was between 60 and - yards deeper to the Cannel Mine, in which the explosion has occurred. This pit was looked upon as being safe. Gas had never been seen in the workings, the ventilation was perfect, and as there had never been any indications from the use of naked lights, they had constantly been used.

Only nine days before the explosion Mr. Dickenson, her Majesty's Inspector of Mines for this district, visited the pit, and found its condition in every way satisfactory. It had been customary for James Holt, the fireman and underlooker, to make two examinations of the workings each day, the first being in the morning before any miners went down, and the second one at noon. He examined the workings on Tuesday morning and again while the men were at dinner, and on each occasion found them apparently right.

There had been two windings up the shaft after the men had recommenced work, and then an extremely loud report was heard over a radius of fully one-quarter of a mile, followed by the emission from the pit shaft of a dense volume of smoke, which completely hid from view the head gearing above. It was only too apparent that a fearful explosion had occurred below. When the smoke and dust had cleared away, it was found that the cage ropes had been broken, and that one of the cages had fallen down the shaft, whilst several of the iron plates which covered the pit bank had been blown up and fragments hurled in various directions, some of them falling upon the roof of a cabin and breaking through the slates. In a minute or two afterwards Thomas Worrall, the bankman, was found lying unconscious a short distance from the shaft having been blown from his post through the upheaval of the iron plate upon which he had been standing. He was removed home, where it was found that he had sustained very severe injuries.

A boy named William Has(-) employed to wheel the trucks to and from the pit shaft was also discovered upon the ground. He had been thrown some distance, and several of his teeth had been knocked out. It is almost needless to say that a dense crowd soon collected at the bottom of the pit bank, many of them being wives, near relatives, and friends of the men below. It was known that about 70 men and boys were in the pit, and vigorous efforts were constantly made to attach a hoppet or iron tub to a rope across one of the pulleys for the purpose of making a descent. The empty hoppet was first lowered as far as the Trencherbone mouthing, and on being drawn up again it was found to contain two men and a boy, named respectively William Morris of Little Lever, Adam Davenport of Kersley, and William Barrett, of Ringley. They were suffering from after-damp, and were attended by Mr. Alfred Kershaw, surgeon, Farnworth, and Mr. Eames, jun., surgeon, whose services been called into requisition by a mounted messenger. Holt the fireman, and one or two others, then descended for the purpose of exploring the workings.

They learned that the report of the explosion had been heard in the Trencherbone Mine, and that the men working there had immediately hastened towards the "mouthing." As they

185

approached it, many of them were overcome by the after-damp which rose from the Cannel mine below, and fell to the ground insensible. These were at once carried to the pit shaft, placed in the hoppet, and wound up. Again and again the hoppet was lowered, until at five o'clock all the men and boys, except one young man, had been recovered from the Trencherbone workings. They numbered altogether 21, and nearly all of them, suffering more or less from after-damp, had to be removed to their homes in carts. Henry Johnson, a son of the manager, had a very narrow escape of his life. According to his statement he was standing at the time of the explosion at the mouth of the Trencherbone mine talking to Thomas Hilton, a hooker-on, and he remembers nothing after the catastrophe until he found himself at home.

As soon as possible after the release of the men in the Trencherbone Pit, attention was directed to the removal of the obstruction which prevented access to the Cannel Mine, and which was caused by the fall of the cage and other lumbers down the shaft. This was a work of considerable difficulty and danger, owing to the destruction of the signalling apparatus, and was not accomplished until close to six o'clock. Nearly half an hour afterwards, Holt and his gallant band of explorers succeeded in recovering the first body – that of the young man Thomas Hilton, aged 19 years, who was employed, as already stated, as a hooker-on at the entrance to the Trencherbone Mine. He had apparently been "sucked" out of the mouthing into the shaft and had fallen to the bottom. One of his shoulders was dislocated, and he had sustained other dreadful injuries, his head being much swollen. His body was sent to the surface and placed in an outhouse near the pit bank. Holt on coming to the surface again, reported that he and his party had penetrated the tunnel which was fifteen yards in length, and had found the air pretty good. An exploring party was formed for the purpose of examining the Cannel Mine. It consisted of Mr Dickinson, Government Inspector, who had been telegraphed for; Mr J Grimshaw of the Stand Lane Colliery, Radcliffe; Mr Woodman of the Clifton and Kersley Colliery; and Holt the underlooker, they found that they could not penetrate into the workings for more than 16 yards owing to the bad state of the air. In order to remedy this a furnace was lighted at the foot of the up-cast shaft, and this had the effect of making the air comparatively clear, so much so that the party were enabled to go into the workings. When they had been down about an hour and a half, without having made any signal to be wound up, great anxiety about their safety was manifested by Mr Stott, one of the principals in the firm and other gentlemen, and an engineer was ordered to wind up. He did so but when the hoppet reached the surface it was found to contain nothing but an extinguished safety lamp. At first it was thought that the lamp had been put out by the gas or foul air, but on examination it was found to have been put out by the action of the air in the winding up.

If possible, still worse fears were entertained as to the safety of Mr Dickinson and his gallant companions, and Mr Martin, deputy Government Inspector, Mr Johnson, the manager and two other men at once got into the hoppet and were lowered into the Trencherbone mouthing. It should be here stated that Mr Johnson was at Wigan at the time of the explosion, and only heard of the catastrophe whilst in a tradesman's shop in Farnworth on his return home, and could scarcely credit the fact until he was shown the report in that afternoon's Daily Chronicle.

This exploring party did not send up any - but soon after eight o'clock a signal was heard to wind up, and when the hoppet reached the surface it was found to contain Mr Dickinson and the other members of this exploring party, apparently all right but very cold, dirty and wet. Mr Dickinson and his companions were heartily congratulated upon their safe return to the surface and then anxious questions were put to them. Mr Dickinson communicated to Mr Stott the sad intelligence that they had been through all the workings which they could possibly enter, that they had seen 16 dead bodies and that no hopes could be entertained for the safety of the others. They added that the air in some parts were tolerably good, but that in other parts it was highly charged with after-damp. They said that they had shouted into some of the workings, which they did not seem prudent to enter, and that the only reply they heard was the echo from their own voices.

The sad news rapidly spread among the dense and anxious crowd which stood in front of the pit bank shivering from the effects of a cold piercing north wind, but who nevertheless manifested a quiet demeanour and earnestly discussed each item of information which reached them. Many of the crowd remained until about midnight, and were only induced to return home when they found there was no likelihood of any of the dead being brought to the surface until the following day. Every assistance possible was rendered by scientific gentlemen from other pits, who hastened to the scene immediately after the report of the catastrophe reached them, one of the principals of the Clifton and Kersley Colliery Co: Mr Wallwork and Mr Bowker, from the Bridgewater Trustees Colleries: Mr Horrocks, of Messrs A Knowles and Co's pit, Pendlebury: Mr Drimham of the Outwood Colliery; and Mr Taylor, from Fogg's Colliery, Darcy lever. The Rev. C. Lowe, MA, a vicar of St Stephen's Church, Kersley was present until a late hour and exerted himself in a quiet, unostentatious manner in - as far as possible the fears and anxieties of those in the crowd who had relatives down the pit.

Throughout the night the work of repairing the doors, -, and other ventilating apparatus in the mines which needed cleaning away the debris which had been blown from the roofs and sides of the workings, was vigorously pushed forward. It was found that tubs laden with coals had been blown over, whilst at the - and in the wagon roads, sides of trucks were found lying, in all directions, having been shattered by the force of the explosion. The men to whom the dangerous task of clearing the roadways etc had been entrusted numbered nearly 30 of reliefs. Their difficulties were increased by the fact that the whole of the workings form an incline of 1 to 3 ft, and are in many places so confined that a man cannot walk upright in them. In consequence of these obstacles it was not until nearly eight o'clock on Wednesday morning that the workers were able to begin removing the dead bodies to the pit eye, preparatory to sending them up the shaft. So rapidly was this melancholy duty performed that by soon after 10 o'clock the number found was 20, which was increased by midday to 21.

Shortly before one o'clock the bottom of the shaft was so covered with bodies that it became necessary to commence the work of winding them to the surface, as the guiding rods and sides of the downcast shaft had been repaired. The remaining cage was brought into the - of the less convenient hoppet. Some difficulty was at first experienced in lowering the cage to the mouth of the mine, but after it had been raised and lowered four more times it descended to a proper depth. It was, however, soon afterwards found that the cage would not wind satisfactorily, and the hoppet was again brought into requisition. At a few minutes after one o'clock the first body was wound up to the surface. It was that of a boy named Enion, and the remains, which were wrapped up in a piece of brattice cloth were carried into the outhouse. After this, the process of winding up one body, and other times two, all wrapped in brattice cloth, proceeded as rapidly as could be expected under the circumstances. A relay of colliers acting as bearers was in attendance at the "tally - cabin" at the mouth of the pit, and on the hoppet, with it's - freight, reaching the top, the bodies were placed – and and conveyed, some to the carpenter's shop connected with the colliery, and some to a stable belonging to the Unicorn Pub.

All the bodies were much burned and lacerated, deep gashes being upon some of the (bodies), whilst upon others the skin appeared to have been literally torn off for several inches in length. A considerable number of women were in the outhouses, and as each body was brought in they at once proceeded to wash and lay it out. Upon each body was a slip of paper with a number upon it, the corresponding number being inserted in a sheet or book which indicated the position in the mine in which the body was discovered. The fearful injuries which the dead had sustained rendered identification by their relatives a matter of great difficulty – in several cases recognition being only possible by means of the clothing or clogs worn by the deceased. Many painful scenes occurred. The widow of Christopher Moores, who resided in Lindley Row, soon identified the body of her husband which was recovered about four o'clock; and she became particularly affected whilst pointing out some repairs which he had effected in the soles of his clogs on Monday evening.

The corpse of George Lindley, between 45 and 50 years of age, and his son Ellis, aged 15 years, were taken into the stable room after each other; and it is worth noting that the poor boy met his death on his birthday. By seven o'clock at night all the bodies except two had been taken out of the pit. These latter were the remains of a boy named Peak and a married man named William Maych. They were unexpectedly found buried among the wreckage in the dib hole at the bottom of the shaft, and there is no doubt that they were blown out of the Cannel Mine. Owing to the difficulty which would have been experienced in extricating them while the damage done to the shaft and the girding rods was only partially repaired, the work of removing them was left until the last.

At one o'clock on Thursday morning, the body of Peak was recovered from the dib hole, whilst Maych's remains were not sent to the surface until five o'clock. Whilst the men were engaged in recovering these bodies they found the upper portion of the skull of one of the boys named Enion. Soon after ten o'clock on Thursday morning the identification of the bodies was resumed, and the scene in front of the two stables, in which the bodies were laid out in two rows, was even more heart-rending and distressing than had been previously witnessed. One woman, in particular, identified her husband, George Lindley, and, whilst in a paroxysm of grief, she espied also the mangled corpse of her son, Ellis, lying in another The Wolstenholmes and Redgraves 1841 - 2002 row. She, like several of the widows and mothers before her, had to be assisted out, and a succession of such scenes followed. Policemen, stationed at the stable doors, held up bundles of clothing to the crowd in front for identification, and the parties recognizing them were taken into the stables to see the bodies to which they belonged, and to have their names duly entered for the Coroner's inquiry tomorrow. By about one o'clock in the afternoon all the bodies had been identified, the following being the official

LIST OF THE KILLED

Thomas Hilton, aged 20, Fletcher's Houses, Kersley; single
Absolom Barnes, aged 14, Stoneclough; single.
Alfred Isherwood, aged 31, Lower Kersley; married, seven children.
Samuel Wolstenholme, aged 47, Lindley's Houses; married, seven children.
Wm. Wolstenholme, aged 21. Kersley Moor; married no family
Amos Lomax, aged 17, Irwell Bank, Kersley; single.
Christopher Moore, aged 26, Lindley's Houses; married, three children.
Richard Featherstone, aged 18, Albert-street, Kersley; single.
Joseph Hobsen, aged 26, Kersley Moor; married, three children.
Charles Tonge, aged 16, Kersley; single.
William Leach, aged 24, Lower Kersley; married, two children.
Thomas Lomax, aged 28, Irwell Bank; married, two children.
Thomas Lever, aged 18, Mount Pleasant, Kersley; single.

John Harrison, aged 40, Old House Croft, Kersley; married, three children

James Beattie, aged 19, Manor Houses, Kersley; single.

Richard Wallwork, aged 25, Jane-lane, Swinton; married, two children.

James Partington, aged 44, Kersley Moor; married, two children.

James Byron, aged 32, Slater-field, Bolton; married, two children.

Thomas Byron, aged 28, Warm Hole, Kersley; married, four children.

George Lindley, aged 47, Kersley Moor; married, four children.

Ellis Lord (or Lindley), aged 14, Kersley Moor, son of the above.

Peter Fogg, aged 26, Clifton; married, no family.

Wm. Morris, aged 15, Tasker-lane, Kersley; single.

John Haynes, aged 21, Manor Cottages, Kersley; single.

John Tickle Lomax, aged 31, Eckersley Buildings, Kersley; wife and four children.

James Hobson, aged 30, Old House Croft, Kersley; wife and three children.

John Greenhalgh, aged 34 (26), Jane-lane, Swinton; wife and two children.

James Chadwick, aged 38, Primrose-street, Kersley; wife and seven children.

William Mayoh (Maych), aged 38, fireman, Kersley; married, and four children.

William Barnes, aged 38, Stoneclough; married, and four children.

Wright Lomax, aged 26, Irwell Bank, Kersley; no children.

Thomas Peak, aged 17, Kersley Mount; single.

Thos. Ed. Mace, aged 19, Tasker's-lane, Kersley; Single.

Thomas Wolstenholme, aged 41, Old House Croft, Kersley; married, one child

Andrew Walker, aged 23 (22), Stoneclough; married, one child.

Robert Clarke, aged 18, Jacksons Buildings, Kersley.

Robert Enion, aged 39, Kersley Moor; wife and seven children.

Jonathan Enion, aged 12, and David Enion, aged 13, sons of the above.

George Booth, (21), Denton, single (started work on the morning of the accident).

Joseph Welsby, aged 18, Kersley Moor.

John Hamblet, aged 31, Seddon-street, Kersley; wife and two children.

George Jackson, aged 28, Kersley.

Kersley Moor presents an unusual and mournful appearance, owing to the large number of drawn blinds. With very few exceptions the blinds of all the houses in Manchester Road and the streets abutting thereon are down out of respect to the memory of a member or members of a family, a near relative, or a friend.

At about half-past nine o'clock on Thursday night all the 43 coffins, which had been well made of oak by Messrs. Coope Bros. arrived at the colliery in two wagons, and in half an hour afterwards the duty of placing the corpses into them was commenced. By three o'clock yesterday morning all the bodies had been put into the coffins, and neatly covered with shrouds. Seven of them were placed in a small stable belonging to the Unicorn Inn, whilst the remainder were kept in the stable upon the colliery premises. They were arranged in rows, elevated about four or five feet from the ground, with the lids reared up at the head of each coffin, whilst under the coffins were placed the clothing of the deceased carefully wrapped up and labelled with the owner's name.

Yesterday morning several of the relatives and friends of the dead viewed their remains, and although they appeared to be more composed upon seeing the corpses neatly arranged in their coffins, it was evident from their sobs and tears that they felt acutely the sad affliction which had so hastily come upon them. Arrangements have been made for the interment of 20 of the bodies in the burial ground attached to St. Stephen's Church, Kersley, today (Saturday). One was interred there yesterday. No interments will take place at St. Stephen's on Sunday. Some of the bodies will be interred at St. Saviour's, Ringley; a few at St. John's Church, Farnworth-with-Kersley; and two at Swinton

+   +   +

Although most people have heard of the Unity Brook Disaster, I've still never managed to work out exactly where the Unity Brook Colliery was! I gather I'm not alone when I read other peoples notes about the mine! As far as I can work out, the pits were located to the south of Manchester Road just south of Spindle point Colliery.

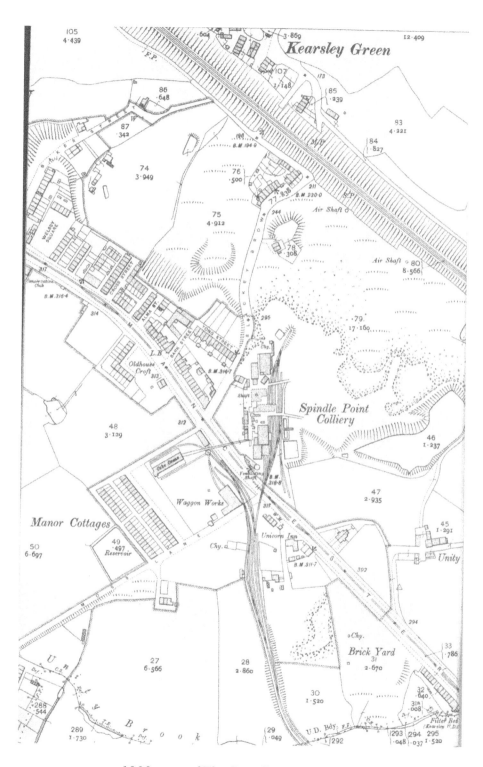

1909 map of The Spindle Point area.

193

Spindle Point Colliery.

I can find remarkably little information about this colliery - apart from that given in *"Collieries in the Manchester Coalfields"* by Geoffrey Hayes.

I haven't been able to trace a SINGLE photograph of the colliery! It was also known as the "Trencherbone Pit" and replaced the "Little Mine" and the "Doe Pit".

What little I can find out indicates that the coal mine was started in the early 1860's by members of the Fletcher family but was then taken over by the new Clifton and Kearsley Coal Company whilst the mine was still being created. One of the shafts had not been sunk in a straight line and one of the Companies first tasks was to "straighten" one of the shafts!

Although the mine was hoping to work the Arley Mine coal seam, it would appear that this was never achieved as below the Haigh Yard Mine Seam at 3621 yards nothing else was discovered despite the No 3 Pit being sunk down to 555 yards. Despite the lack of lower seams the pit seems to have been a success producing coal until work was suspended there in July 1928 and finally abandoned in 1931.

As can be seen from the map, coal was transported from the colliery from the sidings at the mine, crossing Manchester Road and joining a railway line at Unity Brook which led to an incline down to the main line next to the River Irwell. The incline was worked by rope with the fully laden wagons descending under gravity and it terminated at the Unity Brook Sidings at the side of the Lancashire and Yorkshire Railway in the valley bottom. Even after mining operations were suspended, the collieries washery continued in use dealing with coal produced at the Astley Green pits. The washeries continued in use until the around mid 2009, when the Clifton and Kersley Coal Co was absorbed into Manchester Collieries Limited.

194

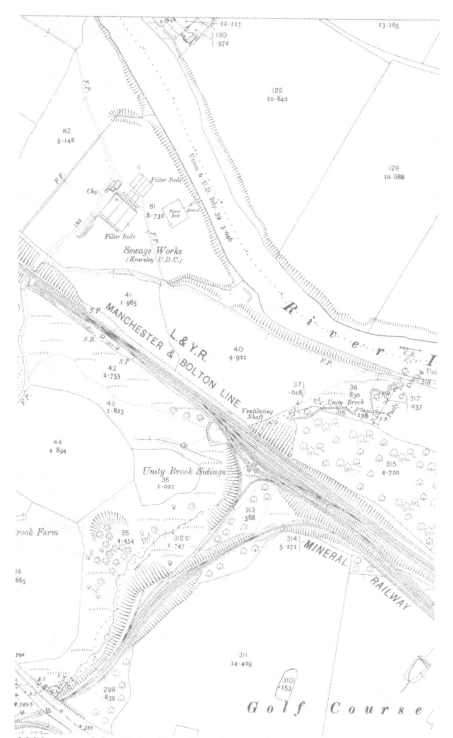

1909 map of the Unity Brook incline and the sidings in the valley bottom.

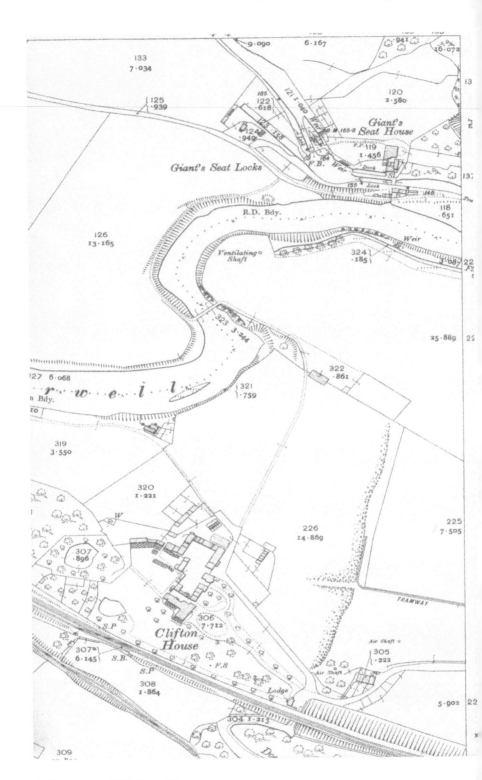

1909 map of Clifton House area.

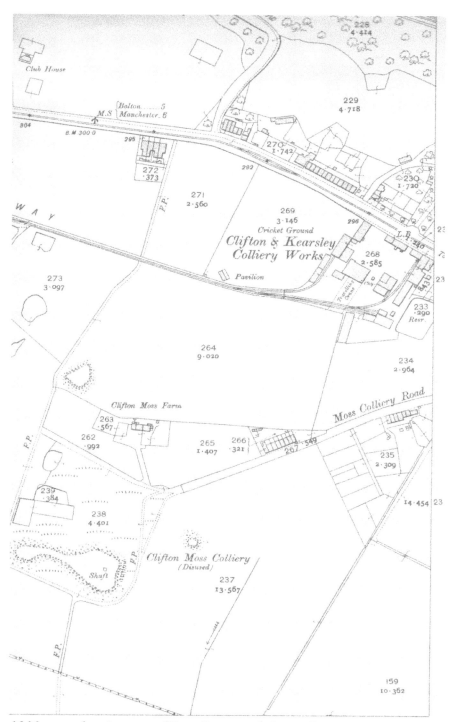

1909 map showing top of Doe Brow and the Colliery Main works and offices.

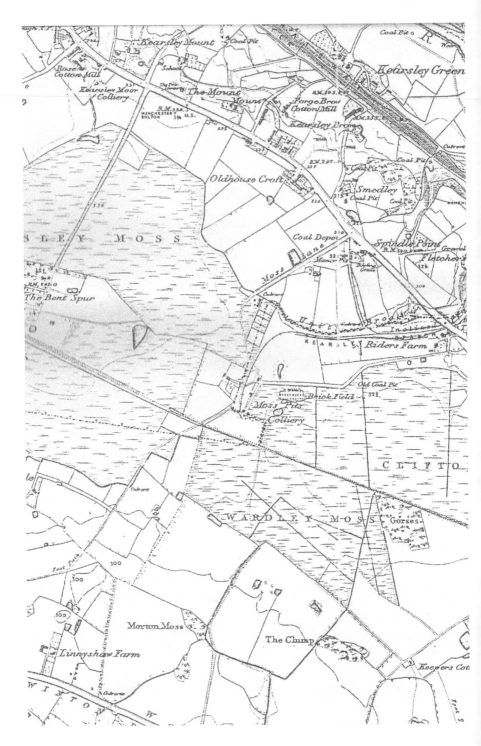

Map of 1850. Spindle Point and Moss Pits area.

Aerial view showing St Anne's Church at Clifton, TA building etc.

Aerial view of Doe Brow, just above the Visitor Centre.

Wet Earth miner outside his Clifton home.

Bridge over Fletchers Canal at Clifton

VIEW OF RINGLEY

VIEW OF RINGLEY. 15.

Ringley. 136.

A view of the Irwell taken from across the river near to the present Giants Seat Nursery. It shows the old "Turbine House" on the Wet Earth bank of the river. The remains of the turbine can still be seen on the riverbank (the Wet Earth Exploration Group excavated it right down to the bed rock but it quickly gets re-covered by river silt) but the building itself has long since gone.

A "pit check" for underground employees of the Clifton & Kearsley Coal Company

CANAL

opt. An interesting view showing

Newtown Pit 1960's © SLHL

Black Horse, Kearsley.

Kearsley Train Station.

Bolton Road, Kearsley.

Bolton Road, Kearsley with Wilson's Pie Shop in Background.

(My great grandma in front passenger seat – Susan Oliver)

Walking Day, Manchester Road
(Opposite Kearsley Precinct)

(shop on far RHS – our family butchers – Susan Oliver)

Cooling Tower Construction,
Kearsley Power Station.

Kearsley Power Station & Ringley Village.

Demolition of the Cooling Towers, Kearsley Power Station.

Canal Breach at Little Lever.

The 'Thirteen Arches' Viaduct, The Clifton Aqueduct and Fletcher's Canal.

Fletcher's Canal Entrance Lock

Coal Kibbles for Loading onto the Canal Barges.

Containers in Boat at the Bury Terminus of the M,B & B. Canal.

Ramsfold Bridge Over Fletcher's Canal.

(L.S.Lowry)

Wet Earth,
'Pit Head Scene', *L. S. Lowry.*

Wet Earth, Drawn by L. S. Lowry.

Ducking the Lord Mayor, Ringley.
(Lord Nelson Pub Behind)

(my dad – smallest boy, 3rd in from RHS)

Ringley Bridge.

The Horse Shoe, Ringley.
(three stories high)

Kilkoby Bridge, Ringley

KILKOBY BRIDGE, RINGLEY

Pilkington's Tile Works.

Pilkington's Tile Works

Pilkington's Tile and Pottery Co. Ltd. Clifton Junction

Turbine House, Clifton.

Canal at Agecroft.

Clifton Aqueduct.

Clifton Aqueduct, 1960s.

The 'Kearsley' Locomotive.

Robin Hood Sidings.

Wet Earth Prior to Excavation of Wheel Chamber.

The end of the Wet Earth Colliery.

This book is an "on-going" project and more information will be added either when I can find the time and inclination - or when someone provides me with more information about the Wet Earth or Clifton area. If ANYONE wants to write a brief article about any particular aspect, whether this be about the colliery, the tunnels, the wildlife, flora, fauna or even the general history of the area just pass it to me and I'll try to add it to a possible future edition of this volume.

dave@daveweb.co.uk

Lightning Source UK Ltd.
Milton Keynes UK
UKHW041255070721
386774UK00001B/168